9-16-68
12-16-68

THE CITIZEN CHRISTIAN

The Citizen Christian

by JAMES F. ANDREWS

*with an Introduction by Theodore M. Hesburgh, C.S.C.
President, University of Notre Dame*

SHEED AND WARD : NEW YORK

1463226

To Kathleen

ACKNOWLEDGEMENT *The author wishes to thank the editors of* Ave Maria *for permission to reprint and adapt material which first appeared in their pages.*

FOREWORD

The fable of Narcissus has been a favorite of poetic allusion throughout our literature. It is a rich myth which unveils certain deep roots of the human condition. I would like to recall Thomas Bulfinch's version of it[1] here because, in stark outlines, it provides analogues for understanding the orientation of Christian spirituality for too long.

Narcissus was a beautiful youth who attracted all of the nymphs of the woods and hills. He was so enamored of himself that he consistently rejected all of the nymphs' advances and treated them with cruel contempt. No one could touch him lest his perfection be tainted. One nymph, as the story goes, called Echo, was particularly maltreated by him and died in her grief. She had tried to touch him.

One day another nymph, who had tried to attract him and had been rejected, prayed that he might some time or other feel what it was to love and receive no return of

7

affection. An avenging goddess heard the prayer and granted the request.

There was a clear pool with no leaves or brush, sheltered from the sun and with grass growing around it. Here Narcissus came one day, fatigued from hunting and thirsty. As he stooped to drink and saw his own image in the water, he thought it was a beautiful water-spirit who lived in the pool.

Bulfinch describes the outcome: "He stood gazing with admiration at those bright eyes, those locks curled like the locks of Bacchus or Apollo, the rounded cheeks, the ivory neck, the parted lips, and the glow of health and exercise all over. He fell in love with himself. He brought his lips near to take a kiss; he plunged his arms in to embrace the beloved object. It fled at the touch, but returned again after a moment and renewed the fascination."

Poor Narcissus could not tear himself away. He pined for himself, could not eat or sleep and finally died.

One of the convictions that has nurtured *The Citizen Christian* is that for too long Christian spirituality has crystallized certain presuppositions which turn Christ's call into a narcissism. Another equally strong conviction is that Christian—or pagan—narcissism is a luxury which our times cannot afford.

Like the beautiful youth Narcissus, we dread feeling and caring; we are lulled into thinking that Christ can be personally loved by will alone, that touch is unimportant. The emphasis has been and is "to save our souls," "to become perfect in the sight of God." Like Narcissus, we scurry again and again to the mirror of our selves with the objective of viewing our actions in the light of what they do for our status in the presence of God. The result is frequently a spiritual schizophrenia which turns meritorious acts into bloodless, unique constructs that have little relation to everything else we do and are.

There is, of course, a delicate balance involved here. We could become mindless actors, unreflective and dead. However, the alternative I argue for in this book is a more creative approach which finds Christ's call a challenge to outgoing acts, acts of concern for the other.

This is not a scholarly book. It is a popular statement written for the audience of men and women who are concerned about living the call of Christ today. The core of the book was published in *Ave Maria*, a national Catholic weekly magazine published for such an audience.

I am grateful to many who have helped me to understand and present whatever there is of value in this book. Obviously, I cannot mention them all, but I would like to thank publicly John L. Reedy, C.S.C., Editor and Publisher of *Ave Maria*, for his patient and generous kindness in "talking through" many of these ideas, as well as John and Susan McMeel, John Chesire, and Father Hugh F. Crean. My debt to my wife, Kathleen, for encouragement

and criticism is incalculable. I also appreciate the work of
Dan Griffin, Managing Editor of *Ave Maria,* for his help-
ful editing of the serial form of several of the chapters.

If this book contributes to burying the spirituality of
Narcissus, it will have been well worth the effort.

JAMES F. ANDREWS

Notes

1. Thomas Bulfinch, *Bulfinch's Mythology* (Collier Books,
1965), p. 105.

CONTENTS

Foreword   7

Introduction *by Theodore M. Hesburgh, C.S.C.*   13

1 Virtue, American Style: Mastering Democratic Structures   19

2 Alewives, DDT, and Living Like a Creature   37

3 Breaking Through Society's Tight Fabric   55

4 Calling Fat America: Your Brother Is Hungry   77

5 Family Life—A Creative Breakthrough   93

6 The Peacemaker   111

7 Heroic Openness to the Non-white   133

8 Dialogue—The Risk of Change   147

9 The Responsibility to Be Alive   163

10 Christ and the Life of Risk   177

INTRODUCTION

The Citizen Christian argues for the rejection of any di-
chotomy between the Christian as religious person and as
citizen. More positively, the citizen Christian emerges
here as a man who has grasped that service is prayer and
who is confident that his mandate is to creatively change
society's structures on behalf of his neighbor. He is a uni-
fied man, without the self-consciousness and twisting that
has marred our understanding of him many times in the
past.

The insight that when we serve for Christian reasons we
pray by our very lives, cuts across the generation gap but
is a particularly dynamic principle among the college generation today. We have a group of students at Notre Dame
who spend the summer in Latin America doing a variety
of tasks to help the unfortunate. Last year one of these
students had an experience which helps put this insight
into context. When he left for Latin America, he was
undergoing a real crisis of faith. Early one morning he was

walking to his duty station, along the shore of Lake Titicaca in the altiplano of Peru near Puno. Early morning mists were rising from the water and he was shivering in the high altitude chill which bites to the bone.

As he passed a miserable Indian hut, a little girl ran out to see him. Down on one knee, he tried to talk to her— difficult because, like her Inca ancestors, she spoke mostly Quechua and very little Spanish. He was shaken by what he saw, a tiny creature with only a rag of a dress against the cold. Hungry, poor, running nose and bare feet, cut off from all the culture of the past and the promise of the future, her lot was a miserably hard life and an early death.

How can there be a God, he thought, if she and millions like her are cut off from all the good things of life that I and so many others take for granted? How can we believe that the Lord Jesus came to save her, if she will never know him or his good message of salvation?

Then it came to him that God or Jesus had to come to her through others like himself, that his education and his profession—he hopes to be a doctor—were both a personal service to humanity and a personal prayer to Our Lord who said: "Whatsoever you do for one of these, my least brethren, you do it to me. For I was hungry and you gave me to eat, thirsty and you gave me to drink, naked and you clothed me, in prison and you visited me."

Education, profession, service, prayer—all became something infinitely more important to that young student

that morning because of a young Indian girl, a chance en-
counter, a compassionate heart and, of course, the saving
grace of God. The Spirit still breathes where he will, again
by the shore of a lake, again in the early morning, but
Titicaca not Galilee, and again to a young man who, like
St. John, was able to say in deepest recognition: "It is
the Lord."

In the present situation, we need more people to come
to this awareness of service as prayer. We have a real need
for books like *The Citizen Christian* which present a
straightforward discussion of the concrete issues which
challenge the citizen today, including racial tension, or the
gap between the rich and the poor nations. There is, I
believe, a felt need to interpret the mandate of Vatican II
in pragmatic terms. The Christian who is not a reactionary
and at the same time is not a totally involved activist frequently wonders how to apply realistically the commitments he is urged to adopt.

Each of the themes developed in this book deserves
praise in itself, but I would single out the author's grasp
of the many facets of poverty and his insistence on a life
of creative insecurity as the hallmark of the contemporary
Christian. Even the theory of this Christian virtue of
poverty has not been adequately developed in our times.
But, as Mr. Andrews points out in so many ways, our practice cannot wait for this slow theoretical development to
be finished.

This is a spirituality for Americans built on the solid foundation of service as prayer. It probes the many Galilees right here in the United States.

THEODORE M. HESBURGH, C.S.C.

THE CITIZEN CHRISTIAN

1

VIRTUE, AMERICAN STYLE: MASTERING DEMOCRATIC STRUCTURES

America and Americans are hard to tune into, regardless of what Gallup and Harris tell us in their polls. The land is so vast and the peoples so varied that distortion is inevitable.

A small example. If you go to New York City, you can't learn its mood by seeing the latest musical comedy on Broadway and eating at the Tower Suite; you've got to feel the pulse of Harlem, the Village, the bedroom communities and the hundreds of other areas of life there. You can't grasp the mood of the nation just by reading the *New York Times,* or *Life, Look* or the *New Republic.* You have to read more widely, including the *National Review* the Chicago *Tribune,* the *National Enquirer,* the New York *Daily News.*

We have joy and happiness in our country, and mountains of consumer goods; my son will eat well today and sleep comfortably tonight. But there are thousands of children who will not, who will fight rats, who will be distended by hunger: that's part of the national reality. There is deep faith and religious commitment within our shores as well as widespread spiritual emptiness. Summer fills our peaceful beaches with fun-loving youth, our inner-city slums with riots. We have all of this in America.

Unfortunately, most of us see only parts of that reality. Most of us don't even realize that infant mortality among Negro children in the United States is higher than among Vietnamese children (45 per thousand as compared to 35). There are loads of other facts, though, that are breaking through in our complacent society—violently—and these facts are making the observer of American society better able to grasp a national mood.

It is these facts that encourage me to characterize the mood of America today despite the risks of error or over-simplification. I think we can at least say that this is getting to be a tough time to be an American, because we are *as a nation* confused about our identity. Innumerable disappointments have dissipated our moral confidence. We are sharply criticized not only abroad but at home. Uncertainty about our society's moral health—something we always took for granted—threatens our sense of security.

We have been involved in a war which has divided us so deeply that our President was forced to seek national unity by removing himself from consideration for reelection. The weapons used in this war (napalm, antipersonnel cluster bombs) have evoked protest within the country and even our allies have questioned and abhorred our actions. For the first time in the history of our country, our young friends, our neighbors, have preferred prison or emigration to serving in the Armed Forces.

We have lived through summers that drained our emotional energies in a way we haven't felt since that burst of violence in Dallas in 1963. Rioting, looting, killing, maiming. Marching soldiers in our streets, machine guns, tanks. We have watched the hope of non-violent progress as Martin Luther King was assassinated in Memphis and even as we attempted to assimilate our national guilt over this shameless murder; and as we held our breath during the spontaneous violence that engulfed our cities, we heard the mayor of Chicago, Richard J. Daley, instruct his police on how to handle looters: "Shoot to kill." Social scientists tell us that these scenes are only a glimpse of the horror of the race conflicts hiding around the corner of our urban slums.

We have not yet been able to cope with our responsibilities toward the developing nations. It is getting through to us that the Western world is the contemporary Dives, but the political realities block effective action.

We have not yet fully grasped what happened at Hiroshima and Nagasaki. We continue building world-destructive weapons, supplying arms to any nation that asks and sometimes forcing them on nations that cannot feed their overpopulated people, as part of foreign-aid.

We can't seem to break through to effective legislation

to control the pollution destroying our great national resources, although this problem is taking on crisis propor-
tions.

We have made little national effort to come to grips
with the meaning of the computer for the future of the
race, although technology is taking away jobs faster than
we can hope to retrain people.

There are scores of other questions that challenge us
today, but these are the chief troubles inserting themselves into our national consciousness and shaking our
sense of identity.

Small wonder that America is in a dark mood, a mood
of anger and frustration, a mood subject to violent
change. But the fact that America is troubled is a good
sign. When a nation's complacency is shaken there is a
chance for new, fresh initiatives to solve problems which
have been around for a long time and ignored because
they didn't hurt. Society is like the individual who ignores
a minor sickness until it festers and hinders daily life. The
fact that we Americans now see that reality mocks our
dreams for democracy and peace could prod us to study
the depth of our problems and look for answers.

So what? What does all this have to do with virtue?
Simply this: It is time for sweeping, radical social reform
to gather momentum, to be painstakingly furthered; the
preparations have been made. To date, most of the energy
for this reform has come from the secular community,
although we now see men of religion, acting in the name

of religion, making a beginner's contribution. In spite of this encouraging, growing interest among persons of religious commitment, the fact is that Christians—and particularly Catholics—are approaching the challenge with a schizophrenia that dissipates their potential. We hesitate on the edge of participation, but our attention keeps returning to the fascination of our own concerns.

What are Catholics concentrating on today? The Church today is on a course which promises to lead it into at least a decade of intramural skirmishes. Consciously, at least, we are "turning inside upon ourselves" *not* to sidetrack the conciliar renewal, but to understand the reason for renewal. Psychological resistance to change is strong and the change demanded by the Council is traumatic. So we prolong it. We linger indefinitely in that zone of confusion where the Church's leaders give in to the temptation of passivity in the face of modern challenges in order to preserve the flock from a sudden wrench which might endanger this faith or scandalize them. Here we are— long after the Council—allowing ourselves the luxury of looking at ourselves—only occasionally coming out of the cave to deal with the real world.

This, then, could be the decade of confusion, when we discuss over and over again the reasons why the Church must change, or explain that nothing essential has changed. And all the while we are missing the mandate of the Council's spirit and documents: The Church has been told to look away from itself, to grapple with the problems of the world today. In *The Church in the Modern World,* in most of the conciliar documents, the mandate is clear. The Church must change because we are not offering a Christian contribution to the effort of solving the challenges man faces today.

Instead the Church in the United States huddles with its intramural concerns. In the face of Vietnam and race riots, our Catholic publications have talked of celibacy and the endless minutiae of liturgical reform. Our "reformed" Church has now surpassed any ghetto Catholicism of the past in its new narcissism. If Pope John opened wide its windows, we have quickly drawn its shades.

We could enter the 1970's impoverished. Unless we do some creative thinking we will sharpen America's dilemma rather than help to solve it. Our identity as Americans is in danger; our identity as American Catholics is even more confused. What can we do to get off dead center?

First, we can widen our vision to encompass the concerns of the world we live in, refusing to be enervated by worries most reasonable men have solved. Secondly, we can attempt to formulate a viable spirituality based on man as he is today and based on the problems he faces today. The best way to do this is to start fresh by asking the questions we need answered.

Such questions would include: What does it mean for a Christian to be an American citizen? Are there special responsibilities that he must assume as such a citizen?

What responsibilities do America's wealth and power place on every citizen? Does the American Christian have to develop new understandings of what it means to follow Christ? Are there new virtues for our time? Does the Christian in a democratic society have to develop new forms of the Christian way of life?

I am hinting at the need for the American Christian to look for a spirituality different from that which he became accustomed to in the past. I am suggesting that a man or woman in our society has special Christian responsibilities that we have only begun to explore. I believe that we will discover that the virtuous life does mean something different in a democratic society. And I am convinced that the last two popes are telling us this in their major encyclicals.

This concept of the virtuous life is based on an awareness of the influential role "society" plays in our environment today. We have progressively become so socialized that the individual can easily feel that he has been absorbed into an atmosphere of irresponsibility and helplessness in the face of mankind's challenges.

Through the genius of our technology, business and government, we have created superstructures or groups—societies—that rob us of our feeling of control. In this creation of ours, we perpetrate acts which will in history be viewed as criminal, as utter sin. We are the civilization, the society, that does not feed the poor, that crushes the power and spirit of those who seek freedom, that exploits whole nations of people, that denies basic rights to minorities. And all of this is done by good men who have not become sophisticated enough to handle the machinery they created, who have not refined their social conscience to the point where they can recognize their individual responsibility in this complex world.

It is peculiar, but true, that the last two popes have recognized what we are talking about here better than the rest of the Church. What encyclicals will Pope John be remembered for? For *Peace on Earth* and *Mother and Teacher*, outgoing documents which speak forthrightly and courageously—even bluntly—about the real concerns of the world we live in. What will Pope Paul be remembered for? For his historic trips on behalf of world peace and world brotherhood, more for his trips to the UN and India and Turkey than for his trip to Fatima. More for his masterful and meaningful encyclical *Progress of Peoples* than for his encyclicals on celibacy and the Eucharist. I'm sure the Pope sees his papacy as directed to the concerns of mankind today and celibacy as a housekeeping detail, an issue that distracts him as he deals with the question of peace, as his heart goes out to those who hunger in the underdeveloped nations.

When the popes beg for Christian responses to the problems of underdeveloped nations, it is obvious that these problems require new responses. They demand that Christians recognize clear moral responsibility in areas formerly unknown and still rather unreal to most of us.

When they seek responses to such questions, they are telling us to formulate new modes of expressing our Christian commitment.

It is easy, then, to see why we are forced to new concepts of virtue. In this book we will not be talking about virtues that can be deduced from a study of the essence of man. We're not talking about virtues in a negative way, i.e., as corrective of man's essence. Instead, virtue is the religious man's response to the challenges and the problems in society. Its purpose is not self-perfective, but instead *creative*. Virtue is an outgoing act of the modern man designed to dominate the sociological facts of his environment, to change them, with the love of God, for the good of the human being.

The challenges that man faces today are not the challenges he faced yesterday, and the responses demanded of the morally serious man today are not the responses demanded of him yesterday. To make the problem even more muddled, man is not the same man today that he was yesterday. He doesn't understand his possibilities in the same way. He doesn't have the same hopes or fears or doubts. His view of himself is changing just as the Church's view and understanding of herself is changing.

In this perspective, then, it is obvious that the virtuous man of today will possess "virtues" keyed to the challenges facing him in his time. We must constantly look at the reality of man's existence in order to know what

Christ demands of him now. And in this view, in this search, in this scrutiny of reality, we may discover the bases for a spirituality that will surprise us.

In other words, our approach can't be the creation of a "model man," but a response to concrete needs and facts. We won't be looking for what modern man most admires. After we see these challenges, we will turn to Jesus Christ to come to grasp the "forms" of his life. These forms will have names that aren't readily familiar as virtues—names, perhaps, like openness and even insecurity. This is not a "for its own sake" approach. We will not seek primarily to be like Christ, but to re-create his presence by living the answers he provides in the historic forms of his life. In other words, our motivation for being Christian will be what we can do for others, not what it can do to us. In the past we have too often emphasized only the aspect of self-perfection, of "saving my soul," of making myself beautiful in the sight of God.

If we must affect the goals and actions of society in our contemporary world in order to have impact, then we must look at the various types of society—family, business, democratic government—to understand how the individual can be effective. However, before we look to how we can influence society or the "group" (and I will use the terms interchangeably), we must be convinced that this is the world of virtue and vice, that this is where we are called to serve as Christian citizens in a pluralistic, highly complex society.

We must insist much more upon the person's responsibility for the actions of the group—and here we are not referring to mob action, but to the actions performed in the name of the members by the group's leadership with the person's active or passive cooperation.

In reviewing the literature on the subject of "society and you," the first thing that strikes us is that the most profound analysis of the individual's responsibility in relation to the group can be found in those writings which seek to explain the outrageous crimes committed by societies that attain, in art, culture, history, literature, religion and government, more than a minimal civilization—in short, by the kind of society that existed in Germany in 1940 or, in a different sense, the kind of society that exists today in the United States. It is the sociologists and psychologists of social crime who contribute the most to our discussion. We will have to take their findings and put them to constructive use.

In *The Respectable Murderers,*[1] Monsignor Paul Hanly Furfey analyzes the criminal phenomena that have emerged from civilized society, such as American Negro slavery, the slaughter of the European Jews and the bombing of the non-combatants during the Second World War (which could be updated to include the Vietnam conflict). And in his fascinating analysis, it becomes too clear for comfort that the greatest crimes of history are "committed with the cooperation, or at least the passive consent, of the solid citizens" who constitute the stable backbone of the community. According to this author, the greatest evils of history—the persecutions, the unjust wars, the mass slaughters, the exploitation "of whole social classes"—are committed by the organized community under the leadership of respectable citizens.

Monsignor Furfey describes the relationship of individual conscience to the standards of society and points out that, although man normally acts in terms of conscience, individual conscience is not the only possible basis or guide for action: "It is equally possible to follow uncritically the example of others, to accept prevailing customs without questioning their rightness or wrongness. Every community has its prescribed way of acting in specific situations—what sociologists call *mores*."

The sociologists have also pointed out that not every society's mores necessarily agree with the ethical-religious principles underlying conscience. If the society's mores conform to ethical-religious principles, the society could be called moral; if not, the society is "paramoral," "one in which at least a few conspicuous mores are clearly immoral. In such societies, the respectable thing to do may be a clear violation of the objective moral law; so that those who persecute religion or exploit defenseless minorities are honored and elected to public office."

Many examples of paramoral societies in our country come to mind immediately: Southern states in which segregation and discrimination have been institutionalized as a "way of life"; Northern states where exploitation of poor minorities by loan sharks is often looked upon as simple credit permitting them to share in the material goods of our economy, and where the unsubtle discrimination of racist housing patterns is shrouded in the pious assertion, "your home is your castle."

How do men—how do *we*—fall into this trap, and what can we do about it? What do the times demand of us in the way of positive, individual actions and in the way of structural changes by our groups, to solve the mass social problems facing us . . . these problems that will be, as we have noted, the blots on the pages of history if we do not tackle them immediately?

We can derive further insight into this question by listening to the psychiatrists. Jerome D. Frank, M.D., published an essay in the *International Journal of Group Psychotherapy* entitled "Group Psychology and the Elimination of War."[2] Doctor Frank discusses—again from the vantage point of human aberration—the psychological factors involved in a community's acceptance of the horrors of war as a valid means for the solution of problems. Rejecting the assumption that war is pathological, Doctor Frank touches on two areas of group psychology as they relate to the possible elimination of war. They have immense meaning for us in our present discussion.

Doctor Frank found, first, that group standards have great power to affect the perceptions and behaviors of group members. The example he cited was the fact that "to Americans, nuclear missiles in Turkey are purely defensive, while those in Cuba are obviously aggressive. To Russians, of course, these weapons appear exactly the reverse."

But group standards not only affect the perceptions and attitudes and behavior of members of the group; psychiatric studies show that they also "give meaning to life." Each member of a group internalizes the group's values, integrates them into himself, and the threat of losing them could represent, according to Doctor Frank, a type of psychological death that many people would find much harder to face than losing their lives in defense of their values. Such an attitude is exemplified in the slogan "Better dead than red."

The second factor which Dr. Frank notes from his study of group psychology is the tendency to form cohesive groups and, in the process, to reject the outsider.

The major point that we would hope to make by referring to the sociological and psychological studies is that eliminating entrenched or ingrained group standards or attitudes—such as those which exist in the United States with regard to questions of race, poverty, war, population, education, etc.—requires basic change by individuals and by groups from *within* the society.

Without citing specific research, we know very well that a single individual in a society defies group consensus only with great difficulty. In fact, the pressure, the power, of unanimous consensus can be so forceful as to make him doubt the evidence of his own eyes. The only possible recourse is a renewed recognition of the value of the human person and a regained sense of the awful responsibility we have as educated individuals to see what must be done and to begin the hard work of changing attitudes and creating structures to effect the necessary changes.

The sociologist Gordon C. Zahn has spent a lifetime delving into what permits a seemingly healthy society to participate in war or cruel exploitation. In his book, *War, Conscience and Dissent*,[3] the essay "Conscientious Objections in Nazi Germany: Martyrdom 1943" relates the moving story of the Austrian farmer, Franz Jagerstatter, who defied Hitler's call to serve and was finally beheaded for his conscientious objection. The story is a powerful study of the influences that "society" and its various subgroups —Church, family, community—brought to bear on a poor farmer-father who refused to deny the dictates of his conscience.

The same pressures exist today. A recent college graduate told me his dilemma: He didn't have the courage to incur his family's scorn and derision by filing as a conscientious objector. He knew what his conscience told him about Vietnam, but he lacked the strength to break through the prevailing mores. He is now a draft dodger.

The reference here to family influence illustrates the extent of the problem's roots. When we talk of "group," we cannot limit it to "society-as-a-whole" but must recognize the smaller groupings of society as proximate straitjackets on personal moral decisions. Economist-statesman

John Kenneth Galbraith, analyzing the corporation complex, shatters some of our clichés about the actual workings of big business in the United States.

What we heard earlier from the psychiatrist we hear echoed by the economist: Galbraith looks at the so-called "technostructures" of today—the modern corporate complexes—and sees that what holds them together is not, as we thought, the drive for profit. What really attracts men to work for the corporate complex is that they "identify with the goals" of the corporation. In many cases, they work there also because they want to alter these goals. The same motivation holds for those who work for government in one or another of its many bureaucracies: "Identify"—the goals are internalized, thereby supporting attitudes and actions. They are mores which may or may not be ethical.

In this view, the problem of responsibility for a corporation's policies and actions becomes more complex. Seemingly arbitrary individualistic decisions by corporate heads are mostly illusory. Decisions are reached by consensus over long periods of time. How do we untangle the lines that lead to policy and pinpoint personal responsibility?

Throughout this book we will return to this theme and explore its many dimensions. At this point, however, we can see that the member of the group today must isolate the major questions and seek to identify the new moral elements that he breathes in. These are admittedly elusive for us—as ordinary citizens—to grasp. We are unaccustomed to thinking in global terms. But we must, because today's problems and the means of solving them are global. 1463226

It is also clear that our major task will be to become effective "community builders," to reshape structures and institutions, to change and alter goals, to help re-define community mores. We must become sophisticated in motivation, in propaganda, in leading persons to freely choose the values that are needed in our time. This is community building.

It is my conviction that Jesus Christ was the chief community builder in history. He lived a pattern of existence or *forms* of life that are timeless paradigms if we but look at his historical existence and search out its meaning for us. He taught truths that were taught only incoherently or partially by others. He gave us an understanding of the brotherhood of men that could change the world if we take it seriously. He preached the first real social gospel. His life was a life of *hope* and *moral seriousness*, two qualities that we will see are essential for rebuilding the world of today.

Unfortunately, Jesus Christ and his forms of life and his message have been shadowed by distortions through the centuries. We won't involve ourselves in the polemics of secularity vs. pure Christian living. We won't discuss whether we should pray or act. These are dead-end streets. We will avoid the dualisms of natural vs. super-

natural, world vs. Christian society. We reject the Doce-
tism which sees material goods and the body as evil. We
reject Manichaeism which sees Christianity as a flight
from the evil of the world. We also reject the ideologized
secularism that sees itself as necessarily anti-religious,
anti-metaphysical.

As men of our time, but in Christ's spirit, we celebrate
the world. It is ours, we are the stewards of existence.
All of creation has been promised redemption by Christ's
life and death. Evil is in the world and its workings because we create it.

Christian existence, in this view, is open-ended. It is
creative because man is creative. It seeks to change, to
redeem. The responses by which it makes these creative
acts in the world are what virtue is all about. Virtues are
creative man's answers to the challenges he has created.
He answers "Yes—you are my creation and I will change
your course."

Notes

1. Monsignor Paul Hanley Furfey, *The Respectable Murderers*
(Herder and Herder, 1966).

2. Jerome D. Frank, "Group Psychology and the Elimination of
War" in *Peace Is Possible*, edited by Elizabeth Jay Hollins (New
York: Grossman, 1966), pp. 91-98.

3. Gordon C. Zahn, *War, Conscience and Dissent* (Hawthorne,
1967).

2

ALEWIVES, DDT, AND LIVING
LIKE A CREATURE

Walk—or rather, run—down a steep incline toward Lake Erie and gasp the fresh air quickly, because the beauty of its promise takes your breath away. From a distance, as you run, the water waves its marvel, it invites you. Then you get closer to the shore and the reality of that lake hits you. You turn and quickly retrace those steps. The lake is so filthy it could make you vomit.

Lake Erie is only one commentary on our lack of reverence for creation. It is by no means the most dramatic.

There are many dimensions to the tragedy of pollution, and the smelly beaches are probably the least threatening aspect of it. It would be impossible to explore all of the dimensions of the problem, since many are complex and some known only by scientific probability. But one thing we are beginning to see is the interdependence of human and subhuman life (animal and vegetative) and the real biological attrition that occurs when the balances of their interdependence are shaken.

To take the example of fish in the Great Lakes, this year in all of the lakes—but particularly in southern Lake Michigan—an extraordinary phenomenon is surfacing: Hundreds of thousands of alewives (a salt-water fish related to the herring) are dying and being washed ashore. According to experts, the situation is even worse underwater: There are dead schools of alewives 20 miles long. An imbalance in the biological interrelationship has exploded in the last two years. The alewives are normally kept in control by the predatory trout (steelhead and lake trout) and salmon, but in recent years the sea lamprey has killed so many trout that the natural death of alewives has been thwarted. The result has been that the alewives are dying after spawning or from other natural causes and being washed ashore. Why are there so many more sea lamprey? Why so few lake trout? What are the biological implications for the human species?

The answers lie hidden in the sea, but some scientists who have spent their lives studying the interdependence of biological life are convinced that man's pollution of the waters is the basic cause. One social critic traced the vagaries of biological life on the East Coast and demonstrated that because of the serious imbalances caused by pollution in marine life there, residents of Atlantic City might someday witness giant hungry squid coming out of the waters to find food.

We are inclined to laugh at that image. His audience did. But the logic of biological balance is really rather elementary. In our age of technological speed, when we can have light by pushing a button, we tend to lose consciousness of the categories of cause and effect. But the reality is there and it goes right on operating whether we realize it or not.

The problem of the pollution of our lakes, streams and seas is only one result of man's contemporary disregard for his role as steward of nature and of the type of priorities he assigns to his options.

Equally tragic is what we have done to the air. Look at the wastes that our manufacturing plants pour into the air daily, ignoring smog devices regardless of the public interest, because they cost money. This, in spite of the fact that industry causes one-third of the nation's dirty air.

No less irresponsible are the cities that have failed to build adequate incineration plants to handle the mountains of accumulated garbage and trash. The present incineration plants simply transform the blight into the worse problem of air pollution; the automobile and similar combustion engines which spill their poison—deadly over a period of time—into the atmosphere and affect the movement of the air currents.

Who can deny the madness of unbridled nuclear experimentation? But though some of the major powers are now restraining their experimentation, thanks to the vision of President John F. Kennedy, France in her eminence proudly rejects the nuclear test ban treaty, as does China in her heady fear and ignorance. A problem apart from experimentation, that of controlling the atomic devices we have stockpiled, was dramatically manifested by the unfortunate incident at Palomares as well as the more recent case in Greenland.

While the world powers can muster 150 billion dollars a year for weapons and defense development to further crush nature, they can't find the 12 billion dollars a year that underdeveloped countries need as capital investment for irrigation and fertilizer. This 12 billion dollars is only part of what is needed in the next 20 years to solve the world's food problems—which the President's 100-man Commission on World Food Problems tells us are biologically, technologically and economically solvable.

A third of the world's urban population does not have access to a safe water supply—either in quality or quantity—though we have achieved man's ancient dream of desalinating seawater for human consumption.

The list could be multiplied indefinitely, taking into account the inhuman ugliness we allow from littering, billboards and junk yards. And these more obvious problems in man's use of nature pass over the more subtle moral question involved in the startling progress of genetic engineering, especially in DNA research which indicates men could take control of their own evolution at a basic level. *Who* would make the decisions? And would there be in this area, also, the profligacy and irreverence that have so widely blighted man's relationship with creation?

John W. Gardner, once a leading intellectual in President Johnson's Cabinet for the Great Society, says: "We can't avoid some alteration of the natural world we live in. But man, even industrial man, is a part of nature, and must find some limit to the headlong destruction and fouling of the natural environment. How much fouled air can we breathe? How much filth can we spew into our lakes and rivers? How much bleakness and ugliness can we tolerate?"[1]

These are questions that seldom find their way into the discussion of Christian response which we call "virtue." As we said in the first chapter, we are viewing virtue in a new perspective: as contemporary Christian responses to problems facing the world. It is our view that the classical approach to Christian responsibility has relied too much on categories that often lack relationship to the world we live in. *We want to respond to our world.* We know that in Christ's life there were attitudes, forms or patterns that are highly relevant to today's Christians even though the specific problems we are dealing with are different. In order to find meaningful forms of the Christian life for today, we must start with the problems and only then look for the answers.

In this view of Christian life, virtue becomes *problem-oriented* and *response-oriented.* Rather than looking exclusively at the Gospels to see what the essential virtues of the Christian life are, we look to contemporary man and his world—specifically, his sin—and we find, after some mind expanding, some grappling with the real world, where man is failing most seriously.

The objection may be made that this is no more than a secular humanism. But the problems are of such magnitude, and the responses required of such heroic frame, that the sustained motivation—the strength of continuing concern and work—will find deep sources of energy in the forms of Christ's life and in the power of the message he has given to his Church. Also, and equally important, as we proceed we will discover that these *are* primarily theological questions.

There is an additional problem involved here—even for the secular humanist: man's general inability to see his personal responsibility in these areas. "Mind expanding," "view broadening," are prescriptions for our time. All too often, we view our life and our environment with medieval eyes. This may be understandable, considering the way that environment has been broadened in the last 22 years: Since Hiroshima and Nagasaki a new world has opened up, a world of tremendous possibilities for good life and exciting conquests, and a world of horror beyond our power of imagination. The A-Bomb and the H-Bomb have changed the rules of war so drastically that even our statesmen have yet to grasp the implications for limited warfare. Diplomacy hasn't caught up. The exploration of space demands new categories, new visions, new insights. The same is true for the public. We haven't yet come close to appraising our American society's responsibility for what happened in those holocausts of the Second World War—of Dresden, of Nagasaki, of Hiroshima.

Why is it so difficult for an individual to grasp his responsibility in these areas? Perhaps we can find a partial answer in the forms of government that have developed especially since the French Revolution, particularly the democratic form as found in the United States. A representative government by which society delegates authority can lead to confusion on the *points* of responsibility. And when government, in turn, passes authority on to agencies and to myriad bureaucracies, it is even more difficult to assign points of responsibility. The same phenomenon is present in industry and in the Church. The result is that our sense of personal responsibility becomes diluted.

This process of socialization, whereby centers of power —political, financial, governmental, etc.—legitimately operate in areas of public concern, forms types of megamachines. In other words, these power centers become supraindividual and impersonal (e.g., "government," "city hall," the "corporation"). The other side of the coin is missed, that just as the individual assigns powers, he has responsibility for the way those powers are used. It is a *distributive* situation. The megamachines refer back to the individuals. In a society that is truly democratic, the citizen has the responsibility to voice his concerns, to use the legal processes to change what is immoral. We have yet to recognize this responsibility, as the actions of

Christians in Nazi Germany clearly show . . . and as our own actions, here in this country, also show—not only in areas like pollution or Vietnam, but also in questions like the use of the A-Bomb and the concentration camps for Japanese-American citizens during World War II.

In a certain sense, then, the supreme virtue for the contemporary man, and one basic to any other virtues, will be an openness to personal responsibility in a democratic society.

As a concrete example of the kind of socialization we are talking about, let's look at local and state government. In most parts of the United States, these governments are using DDT as a pest-control agent. Farmers used it for years because it is cheap and relatively easy to apply. As agriculture became big business, and as local and state governments assumed public responsibility for pest control and also used DDT, scientists became concerned for the public interest and began to study the effects of DDT. The results, they found, are appalling and threatening.

We know now that DDT does not break down chemically when used, that it persists in the environment for years, that it accumulates in the brains and fatty tissue of warm-blooded animals. It can make wildlife inedible. Hunters in the West, particularly in Idaho, have been warned to trim off the fatty parts of deer and elk because of high concentrations of DDT. According to Secretary of the Interior Stuart Udall, "if the levels of pesticide residues in game birds continue to rise, thousands of acres of prime wildlife habitat may have to be closed to hunting."[2]

In spite of the clear and present danger, scientifically authenticated and well known, industry continues to manufacture and sell DDT to government and agriculture. Few government agencies have been prodded into doing something (New York is one of the few states that has taken action). Socialization and the democratic way require that the public—the individual citizen—demand laws to control the use of DDT. Senator Gaylord Nelson of Wisconsin has introduced such a bill which is presently languishing in the Agriculture Committee.

This is a small but concrete case of the problem of personal responsibility in an area where the public interest is pitted against other interests—commercial interests—and where the citizen must bring about a change.

Granted that this is true, what does this have to do with *moral* responsibility? And even if we admit that alewives, DDT, smog devices and nuclear testing have theological dimensions, isn't there a danger that the American Christian will become so involved in action programs to alleviate these problems that he will forget God in the process? Isn't there a danger that he will in his action find prayer irrelevant and God unnecessary?

I bring up these questions here because they are being forwarded by many theologians and bishops with an excessive fear of the "secular-city theology" of Harvey Cox. I think the questions have to be met on several levels.

First, the idea that American Catholics are rushing

headlong into "involvement" in secular affairs is based on a naive reading of the reality. This stereotype of Americans as interested in "action, action, action" *may* be true of the larger society of America, but is certainly not true of American Catholics in relation to their *religious commitment*. In fact, the religious commitment of American Catholics has been so compartmentalized that the social revolution and secular affairs find little creative energy from this quarter. American Catholics *as Catholics* are not in any danger of forgetting a transcendent God; rather they have used such a God as an excuse not to act.

Secondly, I raise the questions here because the problem of pollution and its theological dimensions may legitimately seem remote to many of us. This discussion gives us an opportunity to explicitly draw out the theological aspects, an approach which will be less necessary in other matters we will be discussing. It should be sufficient to say that we should approach these matters with the moral seriousness of Christ because they are human problems. Unfortunately, that is often not enough to motivate Christians because we are geared to a restrictive notion of Christ and his message. We are so accustomed to confining Christ that we mark off only a limited area for our concern and action.

Thirdly, in my halting development of the theology of creation we will see the need for a more cogent expression of the development of a theology of the secular. We will also see the absolute need for our theology to have firm sociological and psychological roots if it is to motivate anyone to creative action.

Please keep in mind that we are not looking for a literal answer in the Gospel to our contemporary problems; the historical parallels are too slight. Instead, we are looking for attitudes and actions which might indicate Christ's *form* or *approach* to a similar problem, his radical outlook which we can, as Christians, make live today.

Our careless attitudes and actions toward the water, food, energy and other goods of the world have deep roots in technological man's view of himself. A warped understanding neglects his creatureliness, his utter dependence on God the Creator. There are many reasons why we fail to appreciate God's action in the world at creation and his creating presence today. But if we are ever to come to grips with our responsibilities for this world—with pollution and nuclear fallout and feeding the growing population—we must drink deeply the truth of God's creative presence.

God the Creator broke through the barriers of time to bestow existence on the world. To cap that creation he evolved man as the king and steward. Creation itself was incomplete just as man is incomplete. Adam's bond with creation was intimate and real.

As the result of man's sin, all of humanity and all of God's creation participated in the radical alienation he caused. When Adam rejected God the Creator, he severed the bond between him and all of creation. This was foreshadowed when God told Adam: "Increase and multiply and fill the earth and make it yours; take command of the fishes in the sea, and all that flies through the air, and all living things that move on the earth" (Genesis 1:28). This was not only a call to stewardship, a call to unity with all of creation, but a clear call to co-creation. Creation itself needed man to perfect it, to complete it, to enrich its meaning, to direct it to the glory of God. It suffered its own loss with Adam's sin, when what God had seen as good, shared in Adam's fall.

Man's intimacy with all of creation is a theme repeated throughout the Old Testament. God's great action in the incarnation is typified in Exodus, when the Israelites yearn and search for the land of milk and honey, when God through Moses leads these nomads to the Promised Land, employing works of marvel in creation to insure their safety: separating the waters and sending the manna. All of these instruments of God's mercy are types of the New Testament's fuller reality.

Throughout the Old Testament record of God's dealing with men we are shown an integral view of man and creation, for example, by the consistent use of created things —animal and fruits—in the worship of God, to seal the covenant and to renew it. David's psalms are a constant hymn of praise for God in which the mountains, the waters, all of creation shout out in joy.

These themes are freshly assumed in the life of Christ in the New Testament. The New Adam has come to reunite man and creation with God the Creator. In the Incarnation God performed the humblest act of history by giving his Son to human flesh. Christ came to redeem, and again—like God the Creator—he makes man his partner. Redemption is as incomplete as creation. Just as to know God the Creator is to become—with him and through him—creators of ourselves, of others and of the world; to know Christ the Redeemer is to say "yes" to redeeming one's self, others and the world.

Creation and redemption are not just linked; they are co-terminous. In fact, they are now the same. In redemption we renew man and the world, we re-create or fulfill what is incomplete. For creation is not finished: "it is full of expectancy" (Rom. 8:19). That is why the accounts of Christ's birth include the stars, the miraculous physical wonders. That is why the mountains groaned at his death, why the veil of the Temple was sundered. All of creation stood still. And today all of creation waits to be renewed by the kindly actions of man.

Because of Christ's re-creating role as the "New Adam," we find his profound sensitivity for the mystery of created being indicated in the Gospels. Christ used these images of nature in every level of his teaching: salt, water, oil, bread, wine. He spoke of the Father's concern for the lilies of the field and the birds of the air.

Contrast our waste of food with the evangelist's careful note that Christ instructed the disciples to collect the fragments of fish and bread that remained after the mira-

cle of the loaves. Christ was the most reverent of men. He
knew God's creative power; he could be sensitive to its
beauty because he recognized, more than any man, the
miracle of creation. One can sense that respect for creation in his plucking of the wheat grains, in the homely
command that water be poured into jugs to be trans-
formed to wine, in his instruction to cast the net for fish,
in his continuing use of analogy to bring created things to
man's attention. "I am the Lamb of God." "Give us this
day our daily bread."

There is a far deeper reality here than the cynical ex-
planation that Christ's only point of reference was his
agricultural environment. The emphasis is so pervasive
that one must affirm that creation indeed knew Christ's
presence and redeeming, re-creating power, that the star
at Bethlehem—even if it be midrashic—pointed to the
hope that creation would not be forgotten in his act of
expiation, his act of bestowing new life.

A few ideas emerge clearly when we look at Christ's use
of nature: He respected nature—when the devil tempted
him to turn rocks into bread, he refused; he respected the
integrity of a thing to be—creation is not to be used reck-
lessly and without concern for its dignity. On the other
hand, created things are to be used: Bread was multiplied; fish was multiplied; water was changed to wine; the
wheat is to be plucked even on the Sabbath to feed the
hungry disciples; salt is to salt food—if it loses its flavor,
of what use is it?

Why have we lost reverence for creation? Why have we failed to respect our intimate bond with creation? Partly, no doubt, because we have lost our sense of creatureliness, our primal bond with all creation.

As we have evolved, as we have perfected our human capacity, as we have come to share more fully in the creative role, our new power has deluded us. This is very much connected with the dehumanization that progresses as we develop technologies of power to achieve control over our natural environment as well as over the human community. Lewis Mumford, the social critic, explains the effect of these technologies when he says that they (mechanical, political, financial, etc.) systematically break down the complexes of relationships between man and nature by deliberately eliminating the human factor. As we mentioned previously, when these powers become more complex, less human, we tend to lose our grasp of them. We have a megamachine which we take pride in.

We have a *demiurge* and in this heady situation—not without some paradox—we absolve ourselves of responsibility. We feel that we are no longer creatures. We have lost our fear of creation, but at the same time we have lost our reverence for it. It is there to be shaped, to be used.

There is a deeper sin here than we ordinarily recognize. At the heart of our rape of nature is the presumption that somehow the megamachine (the demiurge) will straighten everything out again whenever we will it, that we will re-create what we need when we want. But the question insists on being asked: Do we have that kind of dominion?

When we put our despoiling of creation and our disrespect for it in the further context of the end of the world, when all is to be restored as eternal and new, the blasphemy of our empty hands, the toll of our disregard, the sum of our stewardship will find us impoverished in God's sight. This is part of what it means to live like a creature, a challenge that we must take up regardless of the development of our minds, our skills, our technologies.

All of these technologies are good, as are the things of the world. But they need the form of Christ's life for their *human* direction. That *form* of Christ's life, his reverence for all that God has made, his awareness of his creative role and his redeeming work, must find their place in our attitudes and values. They are the stuff of the virtue of "living like a creature." They must, in turn, find expression in our attitudes.

We have said that our life commitment as Christians urges us to fulfill Christ's re-creating and redeeming action. This demands a reverential response to all of creation. As creatures—as human creatures—our response includes projections into the physical world, actions that embrace concrete needs. Technology has advanced the possibilities of that role; it has made our powers of creation almost infinite. We can indeed multiply bread, if we only mobilize our scientific knowledge and procedures. We can bring the hungry millions to the banquet table of life's goods if we are willing to change our government's priorities from arms to food production. While admitting the seriousness of the problem of over-population here and agreeing with the need for responsible parenthood, we can say with certitude—on the basis of sound scientific knowledge—that the alarming reports of the UN's Food and Agricultural Organization could be cheerful reports of plenty, if the people of the rich nations would heed the hungry cries of most of the world.

This theological view was easier for man to grasp before our scientific age, because the man of the past feared nature, feared creation and had respect for its power. Today we have conquered nature . . . *almost.* Instead of recognizing that we have evolved to a more mature co-operation with the creative God in governing creation, we use the created world like drunkards who think they re-create by will.

These questions are far more practical than might first seem apparent. They are daily questions in the world that we live in, whether we have accepted responsibility for them or not. They are questions that come to bear on every level of business and government today. Too often we shield ourselves from that world, especially in our religious concern. We would rather talk about virtues and teachings that don't impinge on our attitudes and concerns *today.* We would rather talk about humility than face up to the local concerns of the watershed association, or the global implications of germ warfare, or the concrete results of defoliation bombing, or the urgent need for enforcement of the ban on nuclear testing and for extending that ban on testing in the atmosphere to a ban on all types of nuclear testing. We would rather think about a new color TV than find out where our Congressmen and Senators stand on foreign aid or lending of capital to underdeveloped countries at long-term low rates. Businessmen, all too often, want to avoid looking squarely at the anti-smog precautions of their companies, and would rather hear sermons on more distant responsibilities.

But we are talking about a Christian life that is problem-oriented, one that looks at man's responsibilities in his world today rather than at a schema of virtues suited to a medieval environment. These are our problems today, and these are the responses or virtues required of us.

Notes

1. John W. Gardner, "Ten Commitments" in *Saturday Review,* Vol. 50, July 1, 1967, pp. 39-40.

2. Stuart Udall, as quoted in "Storm Over DDT" by Frank Graham, Jr., in *The New Republic,* June 24, 1967, p. 16.

3

BREAKING THROUGH SOCIETY'S TIGHT FABRIC

Leslie E. Brown, a 23-year-old from Oreland, Pennsylvania, was recently drafted into the Army because of a "paperwork foul-up." A member of the National Guard, Brown was mistakenly included on a list of Guardsmen who had failed to meet attendance requirements, and thus became eligible for the draft. Despite a series of appeals which were in turn lost in a maze of red tape, Brown, the Selective Service and the Pentagon said, was in to stay.

Fortunately, Leslie Brown was a member of the powerful middle class, and his predicament was publicized. His local Congressman took up the issue with vigor: This was "disgraceful evidence of a callous disregard of the individual and the inability of responsible individuals to unravel the red tape with which they have surrounded themselves." Largely because of Congressman Richard S. Schweiker's appeal to public opinion, the decision was finally reversed, and Leslie Brown has gone home.

Such incidents involving the Selective Service System—

and other systems of government—do not measure well against the sentiments expressed by the former Secretary of Health, Education and Welfare, John W. Gardner,[1] who has often insisted that everything we do must be finally measured in terms of its effects on the individual. He has also warned that although we set out to create a society in which the individual could flourish, we can see that our highly organized society has inherent threats to individuality.

In this chapter we will discuss society's threats to individuality. We recognize, with Mr. Gardner, that "we can't escape size and complexity today," but we insist that "we can design our institutions so that they serve the individual as well as the system." Society must be designed for people.

What happened to Leslie Brown is, in some ways, a freak; we find it difficult to pinpoint parallel situations in our own lives. But, in fact, we share with him the threats of living within a massive organizational structure which catalogues data and creates bureaucracies, which deals with people as numbers and leaves in its wake an ever-growing impersonality. However, these threats make up only *one* aspect of our concern with this problem. The other side is our responsibility to respond to individuals who are equally or even more brutally mashed by "society."

As we noted earlier, in a real way, we are "society." It is our job to refine our understanding of our own role and responsibility in "society." If an individual is crushed by our structures—structures that we create or allow to perdure within the democratic process—then we are responsible. In this discussion we will talk about not only the freak cases, but also the permanent and pervasive structures in our society, structures which we have to change if we pretend to exercise Christian virtue. Here are a few examples:

ITEM: The family of John and Helen Wiseman was only one of many that investigators discovered close to starvation in Mississippi in spite of a generous Federal food program available in their locale. Senate hearings have recently documented that starvation is wide-spread throughout the state. Part of the problem has been bureaucratic red tape, especially on the state level. There is some reason to suspect that the lack of urgency among state leaders is tied to the civil-rights question: One report pointed out that applications for welfare are rejected if a man and woman are not legally married; that Negroes on welfare get only 26 percent of the state's minimum welfare standard while non-Negroes on welfare get 100 percent of the minimum standard; that the state's entire welfare department is made up of non-Negroes; that there is no minimum wage in Mississippi. Many Negroes receive less than 50 cents an hour, and work a seven-day week.

ITEM: Right after the Newark riots, a few busloads of Negro children were brought to a camp for summer fun.

The OEO then decided that it would not pay for the camp vacation. The children were immediately packed up and brought back to teeming Newark. Crushed hopes? Motivation for the cancellation? Lost in red tape. Finally, private funds sent the children back to camp.

Put this incident into perspective by remembering that Newark enjoys the following conditions (as described in the city's application for funds in the "neighborhood program" before the riots): "Among major American cities, Newark and its citizens face the highest percentage of substandard housing, the most crime per 100,000 of population, the heaviest per capita tax burden, the sharpest shifts in population and the highest rates of venereal disease, of new cases of tuberculosis and of maternal mortality." In addition, it has the second highest infant-mortality rate and one of the five highest unemployment rates. If we could put names and faces on statistics such as those describing Newark and what follows, we could see well the needs of millions of individuals in this complex society.

At least 2,000,000 persons in this country need training in productive skills right now, many because of displacement by automation.

In some ghettos, the rate of unemployment is as high as 47 percent.

Seventy percent of today's 23-year-olds had no job training in school and have not completed a college education. Yet 80 percent of all jobs open in the United States require some vocational or technical skill.

Thousands of families are being uprooted in urban renewal. Lewis Mumford, the social critic, warns that if this is continued "you will bring about even more villainous conditions than those you are trying to correct; for you will wipe out on a greater scale than ever what is left of neighborly life, social cooperation and human identity in our already depressed and congested urban areas."[2]

We could continue for pages with examples of the loss of respect for the individual in modern complex society, of the diminishing of the human, personal element as a factor in national and local planning.

But there are even more proximate examples that all of us will recognize. In all of our urban areas, there is less of a community consciousness, more of an indifferent atmosphere, which probably comes with our mobility. There is also a widespread desire not to get involved. The nation was shocked four years ago when young Kitty Genovese was murdered on the street in Queens, N.Y., while almost 40 people listened to her screams without responding. The incident has been repeated many times since . . . and we have no reason to be shocked: There are people screaming for help all around us, people emotionally unable to cope with the hardships of 20th-century urban life. We ignore them. These examples, close to home, harden us and enable us, as citizens, to ignore the systematic mistreatment of individuals on the national and international scene.

There are many ways that we could approach the problem of what society does to individuals, but we will concentrate on what each of us can do as an individual in his own person-to-person relationships. This is important, but it is not enough—for most of us have narrowed "personal responsibility" sufficiently to let ourselves off the hook. We absolve ourselves of responsibility for the decisions made by business or government, thinking that the decision-making sources are beyond our control. In fact, we are happy to abdicate that control—until it affects us. However, we must perceive what "our" customs, laws, institutions and attitudes accomplish in effectively strait-jacketing millions of people at a meager level of existence. What we do as "society" ought to be no less our concern than what we do on a so-called "personal level."

As we indicated previously, we are understanding Christian responses or virtues in a creative capacity, as actions which change the structures of society by concretizing Christ and his message. And if we are to be realistic we must see that it is necessary today to take a broader vision of personal responsibility, to point up the responsibility all of us share for the present structures which may be crushing our fellow humans.

Society is not our scapegoat: We realistically say that every man is free, that he does choose his own destiny. But this is true only within measure. What we must recognize is that to some degree—and this will vary—the fabric of our society, the "total accumulation of structures and attitudes," *does* affect our options and potentiality. We members of the middle class have a more difficult time grasping this fact because our options are kept genuinely open by the law of the land. We are part of the large majority that controls the political fate of the men in Washington. In American society we are not discriminated against; we are all-powerful taxpayers, consumers and voters.

The middle-class child will attend good schools and receive in full measure his share of whatever society can afford. Except in a time of national economic depression, he will receive more than a minimum of goods. He will not fear for his next meal, nor for a warm bed. Not that life is idyllic: His parents must work hard for their share of security, but society does protect his life's development more fully. There is, in short, no need for him to engineer a heroic breakthrough—even though he might feel, in assessing later success, that he is a self-made man.

On the contrary, his life is channeled toward success, as our society measures it. In other words, his access to society's goals is promoted through education, social relations, financial opportunity, job opportunity—guaranteed by custom and law. Our youth is urged to make these goals its own by family, church, school, government. In short, society's measures of the successful life are incarnate, concretized, in its institutions. The fabric is tight; entry to final enjoyment of the minimal is predicated on the individual's ability to utilize his abundant opportunities.

As I am writing this, I have a view of such a neighbor-

hood. Men are mowing their lawns, children are playing
in their pools. Some are heading for the local high school—
one of the best in the state. The streets are well paved,
God's sun is shining brightly. Life is good. There is a
palpable atmosphere of security. The fabric of society in
this little piece of the United States is ready to make room
for the men, women and children here, to embrace them.
There is in this country a network of institutions, of busi-
nesses, of service industries, of churches and—even more
important—of moods, attitudes, cultural attributes, which
will facilitate their integral human development.

But if I leave my neighborhood, I can discover streets
and homes that are totally dissimilar. And this is a city
where poverty is marginal. The fabric of life in these
"other" neighborhoods is unique, it is not middle class; it
has not the same values, attitudes and cultural attributes.
A child from one of these neighborhoods will find it more
difficult to enter American society as a responsible adult,
to enjoy the full benefits of citizenship. The schools are
not the same. The educational opportunities, the recreational options are not the same. A freak of birth. Mere
chance. But the options are different. The vision of possible options is different. The reality is different. In fact, the
options are more than different. They are limited, at best,
and sometimes allow only anti-social choices.

That is the first problem of the society vs. the individual. There are others that will cross these class lines and
that are, in the long run, even more important in their

effects. But we must honestly face this first problem and know in our hearts that the poor have less hope, less possibility of responding to our challenge of "pull yourself up by the bootstraps, work hard," because of the fabric of society. The late Martin Luther King called this a cruel jest when a man doesn't have boots.

Recent developments in technology are forcing inroads into the complacent middle-class remoteness from the ruthlessness and inexorability of society's patterns. It is coming in many ways, especially through the replacement of men by machines. The computerized age is demanding restraining of men in specialized skills, men who were the backbone of the community just a few years ago. Now, at 40, their jobs have become obsolete. Thousands of railroad men have already experienced this, and now it is hitting every type of industry.

Another group are the retirees who, until Medicare, lived in fear of the unknown but ominous future when medical costs would spiral upward. The "Medicare" legislation is a case of middle-class America responding to a common fear, commonly felt. The legislators responded. A *problem* was solved. In this case, the social legislation is not profligacy, this is not "coddling"—this is responsible action to solve a problem. Society normalizes the solutions to the majority's problem. Law guarantees the solution. The subcultures of society don't enjoy these same prerogatives, because, impoverished and disorganized, they lack effective power.

And only now—a generation after his brothers in the factories and shops—has the farm laborer been able to begin to force the industrial unions to concern themselves about his welfare. Disenfranchisement is no respecter of color; if you are poor enough in our affluent society, you will, generally, belong to one of the small, parallel societies like Appalachia.

But much of this discussion is rhetoric and we remain skeptical until faced with hard fact. How does "society" keep the individual from fulfilling his potential? Can this be documented?

Obviously, we cannot explore all of society's threats to individuality. Perhaps we will be unable to deal with the most significant of such threats. But if we are able to document *one* such area, it could help us to see the reality of society's influence and furnish us with some ideas for coping with it.

One man who has contributed substantially to our understanding of how society limits opportunity for human development among the poor and underprivileged is Oscar Lewis, the eminent sociologist who wrote *La Vida: A Puerto Rican Family in the Culture of Poverty.*[3] This book, a day-to-day tape of the actions, attitudes, feelings, loves, hates and prejudices of the poor, grips the reader. It is the story of the Rios family, a story of grinding poverty, of prostitution, of unbelievable forms of human existence here in our own country. What concerns us here is what the Rios family study tells us about the so-called "culture of poverty"—about the way of life passed down in a family from generation to generation, about the structures and institutions which a subculture within society must form in order to survive.

According to Lewis, a certain set of conditions must be present before a culture of poverty will emerge:

a cash economy, wage labor and production for profit; a persistently high rate of unemployment and underemployment for unskilled labor; low wages; the failure to provide social, political and economic organization, either on a voluntary basis or by government imposition, for the low-income population; a set of values in the dominant class which stresses the accumulation of wealth and property, the possibility of upward mobility and thrift, and explains low economic status as the result of personal inadequacy or inferiority.

In the face of these conditions, the poor develop a way of life, a culture of poverty, which is an attempt to respond and react to their "marginal position in a class-stratified, highly individuated, capitalistic society." This set of structures and attitudes corresponds to their attempts to cope with their *hopelessness* and *despair* which develop when they realize "the improbability of achieving success in terms of the values and goals of the larger society." Slum children absorb these values and attitudes at an early age (Lewis says six or seven); and after absorbing them they are no longer psychologically geared to take

advantage of changing conditions or increased opportunities.

The fact that they make low wages and are chronically
unemployed leads to low income, lack of cash reserves,
lack of food reserves, and poor credit ratings. They are
locked out of the larger economic system of society. Some
of the steps they must resort to, because of these conditions, include "pawning of personal goods; borrowing
from local moneylenders at usurious rates of interest . . .
frequent buying of small quantities of food many times a
day as the need arises."

In addition, the poor have a low level of literacy and
education, usually do not belong to political parties or
labor unions, make very little use of banks, department
stores, cultural and recreational facilities. They distrust
the representatives of the larger society's institutions
mostly because of their unsatisfactory relations with police and officials of welfare. They are cynical about the
Church.

The picture that comes clear here is the existence of a
subculture within a larger society; a subculture that, in
order to survive, fashions attitudes and goals that the
larger society misunderstands and refuses to accept; a
subculture that molds those born into it and generates
itself into the future. Add to this the problem that even
members of the larger society share—today's absolute
need for vocational training adapted to skilled occupa-
tions—and you have some insight into the problem of

breaking through to a minimal existence in the larger society.

Not that the culture of poverty has no positive values. It has. We are not, in this discussion, uncritically accepting the values and goals of the larger society. Instead, we are attempting to indicate that the fabric of society is tight and that unless the individual is taken into account every day, the persons we describe here will never enjoy a full human life with equal opportunity for education, employment and the other benefits of civilization. They are "born losers."

Hopelessness and despair are their marks—an inability to cope with the situation, with the threat, that the larger society poses to them. A peripheral participation in the larger society's institutions. A growing awareness that much of what they must fight for is guaranteed to the members of the larger society. A distrust even of each other.

The social scientists—as well as those involved in social work and pastoral work among the poor—can help us discover how the poor can break through this culture to an attainment of the basics of the human life.

Lewis describes the process of change from the culture of poverty to identification with a larger society in the following manner:

When the poor become class conscious or active members of trade-union organizations, or when they adopt an internationalist outlook on the world, they are no longer part of the culture of the poor. . . . Any movement, be it religious, pacifist or revolutionary, which organizes and gives hope to the poor and effectively promotes solidarity and a sense of identification with larger groups, destroys the psychological and social core of the culture of poverty.

This judgment has been verified especially by those involved in civil-rights work among Negroes and by those working with the poor in the slums of South America, scenes of utter hopelessness. The main job is community building, helping the person become part of a larger group working for the same goals, helping people see that by political and economic solidarity they can achieve ends otherwise impossible.

An important footnote is that they must control their destiny in the formation of such groups: That is particularly why Sargent Shriver's ill-fated attempt to involve the poor themselves in the administration of the war on poverty was much more than a psychological boost to the program—it was essential.

Once again we come back to the notion of community building, the need to help people become part of the brotherhood of man, the need to pull back the mesh that separates us, to take our brother's hand and help him recognize the solidarity of man, the utter bond of unity that he shares with you and with me. This principle of establishing hope is relevant for all of our relationships with those—poor or rich—who are having difficulties adapting to society. Hope—helping a breakthrough and helping a person to discover community. Perhaps this is the root meaning in Christianity of the virtue of radical respect for the value of the individual. I would hope that at this point several facts have come out in clear relief about the relationship of the individual to society.

Most important is that we recognize the *fact* that many persons in the United States—in the world—are cut off from effective communication and enjoyment of the values and goods of civilization. Cut off—not by their will, as we have demonstrated, but by the unbending reality of modern societal life.

We have seen the actual conditions that create and foster a subculture of poverty which screens the individual from a vision of his potential in society and which keeps him "in his place."

Throughout the discussion we presume that the reader accepts Pope John's and Pope Paul's basic idea that every human should enjoy the development of all of his human capacity; being educated to his full potential, he should have full access to property and employment, literacy, food, freedom of religion and movement. Equally significant here is *Mater et Magistra*'s teaching that a person's first duty is to exercise his rights.

And then we saw that the best way to combat the culture of poverty is to destroy hopelessness by furthering interpersonal grouping in organizations that bring about a sense of common purpose and unity.

By analogy we have seen also that this principle of unity, of bringing a man into the feeling of oneness and brotherhood, will be the answer to dealing with all who feel estranged from society, rich or poor.

As Christians, our response to this situation is demanded not in charity, but in justice. Helping those trapped in a subculture of poverty to form political, economic and social groups, for example, is not a charitable work but a duty, a creative response on behalf of change in society. We cannot plead ignorance. We must assume the burden of informing ourselves on the structures in our society which hinder personal development and discover the processes for their change.

The problems of those fighting for a place in society are compounded by their invisibility. You and I can live unaware of their plight, unresponsive to their need because we are in ignorance. Michael Harrington's ground-breaking book[4] which opened the way for the "war on poverty" astounds us by claiming that at least 50 million Americans live below the poverty line. When we extrapolate this to the international needy, our ignorance is even greater. One visit to South America alone would be sufficient to convince anyone that the United States—even granting Harrington's figures—is Dives compared to the underdeveloped world.

Thus, one of our most pressing needs is more information, more data about social conditions not only in the United States but in the world. One creative legislator, Minnesota's Senator Walter Mondale, has recognized the urgency for social data and has introduced into Congress a bill which would, in large part, supply the *facts* to cope with our national problem. According to the July 18, 1967 issue of the *Wall Street Journal,* he is pushing for the government to start to develop more meaningful information for decisions on such far-ranging social problems as erasing poverty, improving education and rebuilding cities. Senator Mondale says: "The continuing controversy over domestic social programs reflects a serious need for more refined and reliable information on which to base our decisions." For instance, do our housing programs in our slums make the situation better or worse? Also, in our education programs, wouldn't it be wise to know not only the number of classrooms built and number of students attending but also whether or not we are helping them to read better? This is basic information that social planners in government now lack.

In his drive for more social statistics in order to facilitate national "social accounting" on the social health of the country, Senator Mondale is, in effect, asking for more human data in our national planning. We must derive our motivation and direction for programs from the personal unit in society. If his legislation goes through, and is properly implemented, it could help humanize government operations by providing statesmen with "indicators" that have a human referent—unlike the Gross National Product, as impersonal a statistic as was ever devised.

I do not want to give the impression at all that I believe federal or international assault on human problems to be the answer in itself. At the heart of any national program there must be a deep respect for human values, for the human, personal element. This is what *we* can contribute by communicating our own values and concerns to government and to business. Without this communication, our attempts at social reform will be keyed to societal considerations rather than to alleviating people's needs.

Social critic Lewis Mumford, appearing before the Senate Subcommittee on Urban Problems, lectured Senator Abraham Ribicoff on this point: A massive expenditure of federal monies is not the answer. Such massive spending has succeeded, we know, in producing the atom bomb, rockets, supersonic jets and similar instruments of physical conquest or destruction.

But note—this method can be applied only to those structures or machine assemblages that can be designed without the faintest regard for the human factor, and without any feedback from the human reaction. This patently leaves out the neighborhood and the city. Unless human needs and human interactions and human responses are the first consideration, the city, in any valid human sense, cannot be said to exist, for, as Sophocles long ago said, "The city is people."[5]

The August, 1967, issue of the magazine *Act* contained a moving story of what one young mother was able to accomplish in her own neighborhood. Seeing that one family's children were being neglected, she recognized her *responsibility* and set out over a period of months to befriend the mother and to educate her in love for her own family. The first time she entered the children's bedroom she picked up 18 diapers from the floor, and had to teach the mother how to wash them and how to feed the children. After months of discouragement, and rejection, the mother did finally respond.

Here is a level of person-to-person help that we can all accomplish. It is quite a shock to sit back and take stock of friends, neighbors, acquaintances who are in need —physically, emotionally or otherwise. How do we as individuals respond to their needs? Are we too busy or too occupied? Whatever our reason, the first step is to find out who they are and where they are. "I am my brother." Father James Groppi's work in Milwaukee on behalf of a just open-housing law is an excellent example of what can be done by an individual in society. His is a strong, clear leadership that seeks to force society's structures to bend, to change for the sake of those who are oppressed there.

We can understand our Christian responsibility in all of this if we think about what we have done to the notion of "community" in our Christian lexicon. We have narrowed "community" to mean "liturgical celebration." We have tried to limit community to formal worship by members of the people of God. No wonder some naive liturgists are discouraged that liturgical change has brought no noticeable change in "community" sharing. We do not build community primarily in a Church. We build it in our lives by our actions. Thus, for the Christian, bringing people together in trade unions or other organizations is a concrete Christianizing of his world. He is bringing persons to a community in which they share human goals, where they develop themselves in their grasp of brotherhood.

The man or woman involved in such concern will find strength in his contacts with the historical and sacramental Christ. He will cause Christ to live in our time in a personal, real way by concretizing Christ's message today. This can be done in voter-registration drives, in programs designed to get individuals to join political parties, in PTA sessions, in bridge groups, in any human association where persons communicate with each other, where the person is reached out to, where the aim is the formation of human community.

The name of the virtue, in short, is concern or care for the individual, and the action is community building. In a brilliant new book, *A Catalogue of Sins*, William F. May, a Presbyterian minister, calls its lack the "sin of neglect" —the sin against the needy. He calls this sin the opposite of the sin against the enemy: "The enemy occupies the center of attention; he becomes an obsession. But the needy, at the other extreme, barely exists. He camps out at the very perimeter of consciousness. Sin, in this case, is not a matter of obsession but of indifference and neglect."[6]

We could also characterize the sin as "treating persons as objects." Instead of welcoming interpersonal relationships, we gaze at them impersonally and *objectify* "it" as a problem to be solved by someone else or by an agency. This objectification is, as we have noted, a constant risk in society's attempts to help the needy cope with the problems that society has created. But the risk must be taken, for the societal and complex nature of human problems today can be regretted but not wished away. The machines of our society can be programmed toward national and international solutions for human, personal needs if we make the effort. The touchstone must always be the person. The middle class must always be on guard against the arbitrary bureaucratic decision that diminishes the human, that allows the machinery of state or business to ignore human, personal factors.

It would be tragic if we let the complexity of the problem of reorienting the structures of society scare us away from our responsibility. The *human* factor—in the present direction of our society—is becoming less and less visible. The momentum has begun and is careening in a fast course. Now is the time to fight, to make Christ and his message present by restructuring, by rebuilding society's goals and policies.

Notes

1. John W. Gardner, "Ten Commitments" in *Saturday Review*, Vol. 50, July 1, 1967, pp. 39-40.

2. Lewis Mumford, "Why Experts Are Wrong in Their Prescriptions for Cities" in *The National Observer*, May 1, 1967, p. 22.

3. Oscar Lewis, *La Vida* (Random House, Inc., 1966), pp. xliii, xliv, xlvi, xlviii. © Copyright 1965, 1966 by Oscar Lewis.

4. Michael Harrington, *The Other America* (Baltimore, Md.: Penguin Books, 1966).

5. Lewis Mumford, *op. cit.*

6. William F. May, *A Catalogue of Sins* (Holt, Rinehart and Winston, 1967), p. 101.

4

CALLING FAT AMERICA:
YOUR BROTHER IS HUNGRY

"Food, glorious food," sings the street urchin in *Oliver*— and I, for one, would heartily join in that song. In the United States at this moment in history it is easy to indulge that love.

I'm forced to that confession by the size of my own waistline. There comes a time in writing about virtue for the modern man when the writer must take a look at himself. Every occupation has its hazards, and my present topic demands an honesty that could benefit both you and me, if it leads us to glimpse the reasons we are so blissfully unconcerned by the fact that at least two-thirds of our brothers throughout the world are hungry.

The glimpse of understanding will come, hopefully, as we talk about the virtue of "Christian insecurity" and relate it to our ideas about the right to private property.

There are reams of statistics available to dramatize the problem of hunger. Of every six babies born in Northeast Brazil, for example, three die in their first year of life; by age four, only two are left. In most of Southeast Asia, nearly half of the children die in the first four years. Diseases are the cause—but they are minor diseases which could be controlled if it were not for malnutrition. The same proportion of deaths is not reached in the United States until age 60 (statistics from *Foreign Affairs,* October, 1967, p. 126).

The situation in the United States—while less dramatic statistically—is also serious. Most of us find it hard to believe that anyone could be starving here. However, recent studies prove that hundreds of thousands of Americans—according to Senator Joseph Clark of Pennsylvania, as many as four million—are suffering from malnutrition and literally starving. They exist in every city—yours and mine. One example: Doctors who examined 700 children in Mississippi described conditions of nutrition as "appalling"; one, who had worked in primitive Africa, found the situation as bad as anything he had seen there.

Even this information leaves many of us cold, but since the hungry are invisible it will have to suffice. We just don't see or experience hunger, especially in the United States—our society is such that the worlds of rich and poor, of comfort and misery, touch but fleetingly, if ever.

Senator Robert Kennedy was shaken by his tour of Washington, D. C., which included thousands of hungry children in the shadow of his office in our nation's Capitol Building. His first brush with hunger had been in South

America, and now he found his neighbors in worse condition.

But those of us who haven't been to South American slums, who haven't walked in the Capitol's shadow, haven't been stared at by the eyes of hunger—how can starvation touch our lives?

The North American continent is a huge table, filled with good things, things that make your mouth water— like a stuffed turkey with all the trimmings—and Americans, many Americans, sit eating, ignoring the cries of millions. Who cares to strain to listen to the cries?

An indicator of how insensitive we really are is the fact that under the big table are millions of Americans asking for crumbs. And they are ignored.

Now *that's* the reality. Like it or not. If any of us beheld hunger up close, yet saw a family stuffing itself, ignoring children with distended stomachs lying on the ground begging for enough to stay alive, we would call the family "insensitive pigs" and provide the food for the children— even by force.

You're properly skeptical about the possibility of such cruelty. When we do read or hear of someone callously denying another the essentials of life, it is a freak, an aberration which we abhor. On the person-to-person level, the problem is rarely encountered by most of us.

That's why the problem of hunger in the United States and in the world is an excellent example of how we fail to see our responsibility for a social problem. It illustrates again the way we absolve ourselves of responsibility within a complex society, consoling ourselves with the thought that society will take care of the problem. A worse problem is that most of us simply do not believe that the problem exists.

We disbelieve because we trust in the generosity of the Western nations, particularly in our American foreign-aid appropriations. It is true that our country has not entirely ignored the needs of the developing countries—but it is true, too, that our present programs are inadequate and largely self-serving. "Self-serving," because they often have strings attached which require, for example, purchases of American arms and other goods.

Aid from the rich Western nations presently trails the actual needs of the developing nations. And worse: The total volume of aid in 1966—both private and official—was less than that in 1965; the Big Four total for 1966 was below what these four nations (the U.S., France, Britain and West Germany) "gave" in 1961. In 1967, Congress passed the lowest foreign-aid bill since World War II. It is surprising to note how little aid actually comes from the Western nations: only about 11.5 billions, while the defense budgets of these same nations total about 160 billions—roughly 14 times their total aid.

Of this total of 11.5 billions, four billion dollars is private investment in industrial and commercial development, while 6.5 billions is official, government-to-government aid and about one billion dollars is made up of loans from world and regional banks. What these figures don't show is that the poor countries pay about four billion dollars to the rich nations in interests and profits every year.

American sources send about five billion dollars a year to the developing countries—a misleading figure, unless we look at it in terms of our capacity. *Interplay,* an inter-Atlantic magazine which looked at this question from a strictly economic point of view in its August, 1967, issue, noted that the United States is putting little investment capital into the countries of Asia, Africa and Latin America—the future's great market for the goods of developed Western countries. It said that "the U. S. has done less, in proportion to its abilities, to make financial resources available to these underdeveloped areas than France and the United Kingdom."

President Johnson has been concerned about this gap. In 1966, he appointed a distinguished 100-man panel to study the needs of the developing countries.

The government published its report in 1967. It said that "a solution to the world food problem during the next 20 years is biologically, technically and economically possible." It went on to point out that it may not be possible politically, unless the "American people are convinced that efforts merit investment of their taxes" and unless Americans have confidence in the programs and in the administrators of the programs. One of the requirements, according to the panel, is an annual investment of at least 12 billions in capital outlay for agricultural needs alone.

We must not be too eager to cite isolated errors in planning and judgment, or the occasional abuse of aid money, to justify curtailing or cancelling the programs. Some statesmen, such as Senators Eugene McCarthy, Robert Kennedy and William Fulbright, warn that a new isolationism threatens to cut foreign aid to a trickle within a few years—at a time when social justice as well as our national interest demands a generosity unequalled in the past.

Why is our legislative response to the needs of fellow Americans so stingy? Why are we so receptive to any evidence, no matter how shaky, to shore up our selfish attitudes toward foreign aid?

At this point, you should be getting the same flat feeling of dread that I have, because we know it's time to look within ourselves for the basic causes of our selfishness as a society. There is little point in lingering further on the fact of world hunger: We know that it exists. Why, then, knowing that it exists and knowing that it lies within our power to root it out, do we permit it to continue?

The answer is related to the Western world's capitalistic approach to life and work and nature, to a tradition in common law enthroning the right to private property, to an obsession with the right to hold the world's goods; and we have accommodated our theology of the world to this approach, tradition, and obsession.

Christ spoke incisively on wealth, but Christianity has had plenty of time to dull the edge of his words. Today, in America, we hold "security" in high esteem, little recalling the many times Christ called this drive for "security" foolish and nearsighted. Remember his story of the man who kept building warehouses for his grain . . . only to die on the night he completed the project?

If we used to understand virtue to mean building up peace of soul by making ourselves perfect, today we must see that it demands that we shake loose some of that material and spiritual comfort and open ourselves to risk.

We can see why we were slow to respond to the challenge of world hunger by examining the "right to private property," and by looking at the teachings of the recent Holy Fathers on this point. We will discover, to our dismay, that we have canonized the right to private property out of all proportion to the *prior* and limiting right of *all* men to the decent necessities of life.

In *Mater et Magistra*,[1] Pope John pointed out the derived nature of the right to private property in very clear terms:

The right of every man to use [material goods] for his subsistence is prior to all other rights of an economic nature, even to the right of private property. Undoubtedly, . . . the right of private property is also a natural right. Nevertheless, in the objective order established by God, this right should be so arranged that it does not hinder the satisfaction of the unquestionable need that goods, which God created for all men, should flow equitably to all, according to the principles of justice and charity.

Pope John is underlining the distinction between the "right of usage" and the right of "owning private property." He is careful to indicate that man has the right to private property, but it is a derived right. The basic truth is that whatever we own—our house, our food, our luxuries—is ours for use and ownership, but not in an absolute way. We have a right only to what we reasonably need; everything else is available for the common good.

Pope Paul puts it even clearer in *Populorum Progressio*.[2] Quoting Saint Ambrose, he says that when you give to the poor, "you are not making a gift of your possessions to the poor person. You are handing over to him what is his. For what has been given in common for the use of all, you have arrogated to yourself. The world is given to all, and not only to the rich."

Pope Paul goes on to explain what this means in the concrete: "That is, private property does not constitute for anyone an absolute and unconditioned right. No one is justified in keeping for his exclusive use what he does not need, when others lack necessities. In a word, according to the traditional doctrine as found in the fathers of the Church and the great theologians, the right to property must never be exercised to the detriment of the common good."

As if suspecting that most of us will nod and say "how nice—but he can't be serious," he continues: "If certain landed estates impede the general prosperity because they are extensive, unused or poorly used, or because they bring hardship to peoples or are detrimental to the interests of the country, the common good sometimes demands their expropriation."

The sleeper in this statement on expropriation is that it is only one example of the application of the principle that no one is justified in keeping what he does not need, when others lack necessities. The principle can legitimately apply to my possessions or yours, if they exceed the reasonable needs of our condition of life.

American reaction to Pope Paul's remarks on private property was swift: *Time* said it "had the strident tone of an early 20th-century Marxist polemic." The *Wall Street Journal* described it as "warmed-over Marxism." The religious press praised it, as did Catholic bishops and priests. The trouble is that only such observers as *Time* and the *Wall Street Journal* and William Buckley caught its revolutionary fervor and the intensity of its demands for reform.

It is, probably, too much to hope that the principle will ever be applied *fully* in the Western world without force or threat of force. But it touches, too, on the future disposition of the world's riches—for example, of the vast and untapped resources of the oceans. The wealth of mineral resources, of food, water and energy is incalculable; the deposits in coastal waters alone could conceivably bring prosperity to many underdeveloped nations.

World powers are beginning to see the implications of this wealth, and disputes are beginning to multiply. Here is a concrete case for the implementation of Pope Paul's principle. The World Peace Through Law Conference, which met last year in Geneva, suggested that the United Nations General Assembly take jurisdictional control over ocean resources, except for extraterritorial waters and continental-shelf fishing rights, before there develops a submarine variety of colonialism which leads to an international race to appropriate the sea bed. The Conference's suggestion was backed by several editorial commentators, including the *Christian Science Monitor* which saw this plan of financial value for funding the work of the United Nations as well as the developing countries which it assists.

This is not "warmed-over Marxism." It is true humanism. Putting it into practice requires a more drastic rethinking and reshaping of society's goals and attitudes than any Communist ideal could demand.

Your first reaction is probably similar to my own: Impossible—people can't change their thinking that much. Can we, in our wildest moments, consider American Catholics giving away what they don't need so as to help those in India? Can we imagine the Church in this country abandoning its superfluous building programs? Hardly, when you consider the surprise that met Fulton

Sheen's recent decree levying a tax of one percent on parishes that build schools and churches in his diocese. The tax will be used for helping the poor in foreign lands. *One percent!* To date, the pope himself has taken only token steps to lead the way in this; the Church's teaching on this point is not credible in our time. When we release our hard grasp on the riches of the Vatican, when we stop building to serve ourselves, when we start in an organized way to go beyond tokenism, then perhaps we will have a change.

Another major reason we American Catholics feel as we do about property is that we've seldom been faced with a living witness to poverty—to a poverty inspired by love of Jesus rather than forced by deprivation. The so-called "vow of poverty" has been watered down so that in our time it means a mere pledge of individual non-ownership, under which religious publicly vowed to poverty often live better than the people they serve. Fortunately, today's Catholics are seeing this arrangement in a realistic light; no longer will they be lulled into thinking that this is the Christian attitude toward wealth.

Normally, the next step is to absolve ourselves of responsibility. After all, be reasonable—how many of us can send a shipload of wheat to India? Who has the influence to arrange a loan for a country struggling toward development?

But in fact, if the responsibility does not belong to the American citizen, whose is it? Where, in fact, do our elected officials get their power? From the citizen. And to the extent that you and I refuse to face up to reality, to that extent will our government keep its head in the sand.

It is our responsibility, as American Catholics, to change our nation's policy for three reasons:

1) the duty of human solidarity—the same sense of unity that moves us to help a child, any child, without asking who its parents are, when we see a need;

2) the duty of social justice—for example, making sure that strong nations such as ours do not take advantage of weaker nations in trade and commerce;

3) the duty of universal charity—in Pope Paul's words, "the effort to bring about a world that is more human towards all men, where all will be able to give and receive, no group making progress at the expense of another."[3]

For the person who wants to make Christ present in contemporary society, the virtue of "Christian insecurity" is essential. The man who lives this virtue will spend himself convincing fellow Americans that material creation is public before it is private—that property is *first* for the use of all. This is a basic Christian posture because it witnesses to hope that comes from Christ's Resurrection, the hope for a future glory where true security will be known.

What is becoming clear again is the claim that contemporary virtue makes on the individual's security. Virtue in our time calls us to insecurity. It says: "Take the risk of peace." It says: "Take the risk of emptying your warehouses and give to those who hunger." It says: "Take the risk of lending and giving capital to the underdeveloped."

The theme throughout is that the individual must empty himself as Christ emptied himself. The style is different—martyrdom isn't asked for. Rather, Christ asks us to give ourselves to change society's structures, to stand up in the face of group consensus and deny the predominant values, to say: "No, I will not worship myself, my country, my superfluous wealth. I will open myself to the needs of others."

The virtue of "Christian insecurity" finds many targets in our society. Voluntary insecurity for the sake of a brother in need can be the guide-line in a variety of public and private policies. Here are a few instances.

The need to change public opinion on foreign aid is clear from the Congress' growing insistence on tying strings to all aid, e.g., by insisting that a major percentage be spent on arms or goods manufactured in the United States. Another indicator: In two years, the total amount of aid available will necessarily go entirely for fertilizer to meet the food needs of the growing populations.

An indication of the inadequacy of American welfare programs can be gleaned by looking at the population of Washington, D.C., the nation's capital. One-third of the population there exists at little more than subsistence level. Fifty-one percent of the children receive a free lunch at school—not surprising, since a family of 13 on welfare received $228 a month for food, 19 cents a meal for each.

By promoting scientific research, society can help solve the problem of hunger. Government, private industry and education should be encouraged to fund more generously basic research in agricultural technology. This involves diverting funds from research in nonessential luxuries (cosmetics, arms and germ warfare) to essential research in weather, fertilizer, protein supplements, etc.

Some advances have been made. E. R. Squibb Co. claims that the animal husbandry research it started in Latin America 25 years ago is now paying off both for the Latin Americans and for the company. The great advances that have been made with even the limited research being done prove what is possible. A Norwegian firm has a new high-protein fish paste which can be sold cheaply; Peru and Chile are producing a protein-rich food fishmeal; in 20 years American farmers have learned how to get 72 bushels of corn per acre rather than 33.

There is a critical need to stabilize the economies of developing countries. This can be done by ending unfair tariffs that take advantage of the developing countries' dependence on the export of a single product. A case in point: The United States is about to put an import duty on Brazilian instant coffee because American manufacturers are angry that Brazilians are building their own plants to process it. The Alliance for Progress encourages Brazilians to process their own products and they have done it successfully, only to be threatened now with an import tax that will wipe out their gains. The man who believes in "Christian insecurity" can fight unfair tariffs and also buy the foreign product—even if it's unfairly priced higher.

Responsible parenthood can be a decisive factor. Attempts to educate all persons in the dignity of parenthood and in the obligation to exercise it responsibly are only beginning. Barriers to this education and the opportunity for free choice are now breaking down. Catholics should lead in presenting the values of responsible parenthood, in emphasizing the importance of caring about the quality of life of those now living, and in educating all in the elements which must be present in an informed judgment on the question. At the same time, the double character of this right must be protected: Parents are free to make the judgment to *have* more children, as well as to decide to limit their family's size.

Other personal possibilities exist. The man who wants to help his brother can dig into his pocket and support programs that help the destitute—both locally and internationally. This would include such programs as CARE, the Catholic Near East Welfare Association, *Caritas Internationalis,* among others.

If we are young and healthy and have a skill which can be used in the developing countries, we can give a few years or our whole life to service where we are needed. In addition—wherever it is possible—we can encourage the

formation of unions, credit co-ops and other intermediate
agencies among the poor which give them political and
economic power.

It is on the personal level that this virtue must be lived.
A personal choice of "Christian insecurity" will seek to
communicate this value in all the public media, as well as
in conversation in the living room.

That's a mouthful. But all these steps are within the
reach of the religiously concerned man. And if virtue is a
Christian response to contemporary human problems, this
is where we must start. When Christians start doing something about these things, then we can talk about some of
the more "traditional" virtues, like humility and prudence.

Apparently, "humility" will have to wait for a while,
while we proudly do something about starving people.

Notes

1. *Mater et Magistra* (Chicago: The Discoverers Press, 1962),
pp. 19-20. The translation is based on the English text released
by the Vatican. The consultant on the text was the Very Rev.
Daniel M. Cantwell.

2. *Populorum Progressio* (*On the Development of Peoples*).
Translation of Press Department of U. S. Catholic Conference.
Published in booklet form by Our Sunday Visitor, Inc., Huntington,
Ind., 1967, par. 23, p. 13.

3. *Ibid.*, par. 44, p. 21.

5

FAMILY LIFE
—A CREATIVE BREAKTHROUGH

We have been formulating a fresh concept of virtue: Christian response which looks outward, responding to needs and problems in society rather than concentrating on self-perfection. Instead of looking at virtue primarily for the sake of benefiting ourselves, we insist that virtues are creative acts that change our environment, acts which make Christ present for the good of other human beings.

Traditional spirituality focused our efforts on our own development as the chief good to be obtained from virtuous acts. There is something unreal about this approach. It requires us to turn our backs on the way we really live. It separates virtue from our real lives.

Therefore, instead of writing this in a den behind closed doors—with relative silence and a coffeepot—I'm moving into the family room—with "Snoopy Sniffer," "Mr. Duck," blocks, bottles and the jumble of other playthings and their owner, my 14-month-old son. Another who shares my new writing location is my pregnant, harassed wife,

getting ready for an influx of friends and relatives for the
first weekend of Notre Dame football. Before this appears
in print, it will undergo the immediacy test, be marked
with jam fingers, and be lost and found a couple of times.

It is in the family relationship of wife, husband and
children that we are most fully human, that we see the
dynamics of love most clearly, that we know what we are
capable of in terms of loving, and giving, and receiving.
Any spirituality, any approach that pretends to tell us
what is the best way to God, must look long and hard at
what we know of love in the family. Even though we have
understood God in our tradition in familial terms, calling
God "Father" and conceiving the "Holy Spirit" as eter-
nally generated by the mutual love of the Father and the
Son, we have, in fact, left it on a relatively theoretical
level. These formulations have been pure, sacral rhetoric.
They have not touched morals.

We can test the practicality of our concept of virtue in
terms of the family, and we can explore what new possibilities there may be for the family in society.

A family is a "we." Unlike any other group, the family
evokes and thrives upon the most elemental human drives.
It is the most fundamental human grouping, the unit
where man and woman express the best (and sometimes,
the worst) possibilities of human social existence. All
other groupings, in business or in government, will be
human, worthwhile and good, to the extent that they re-
flect the real values of the family.

In the family we may glimpse the meaning of brotherhood. In the family we may see the meaning of unselfish love, of giving, of selfless devotion. In the family we also see the person's need for security, for love, for protection, for privacy, for self-fulfillment. These healthy, necessary, human values must be balanced and integrated into the family "we."

In the family we also learn the ambiguity of being human, for we see the ability of man and woman to betray, to hate, to ruin what is beautiful, to love in order to possess, to be selfish, to be unfeeling and insensitive. In the family we can see how a "we" can become closed, can shut out the larger society, how a "we" can die because it depends on itself alone for growth and life.

But most basically, the family shows us that care for another is a human thrust, that risk in love is a human trait. In the love of a man and a woman, in their mutual giving in vows, there is a risk that is terrible, a risk of giving that cannot be duplicated anywhere. In marriage, man and woman open to each other, knowing *the fact* that their gift to each other can be used, mocked—or even rejected. No gift involves as much risk as the gift of oneself to another human being. No opening or unveiling can match the sharing of knowledge and intimacy in marriage.

And in children, completely dependent on their parents and totally trusting, we see the fruit of love. The parents' gift to each other, in intercourse of love, expresses itself in a new human being.

The whole dynamic of a marriage and a family is outgoing, *an endless series of creative acts that benefit first the person loved,* that find their meaning in the other— the wife, the child.

In marriage, these consciously chosen creative acts, the acts of love that are expressed by cleaning carpets, or providing the food each week, or paying the mortgage, or working to give the members of the "we" a more human life—these are virtuous acts in their most basic environment. And in these virtuous acts, the fathers do not look at themselves to see how they have been perfected, how they have received. They know that a fullness of life accrues to them, a fullness of life that demands, that can hurt.

It can hurt because the family is a union of humans, with all of the changes in temperament, physical reactions, flashes of joy, anger and sorrow that come with being human. I do not find it embarrassing to admit that the members of my family are not always on the same emotional and psychological wavelength. It takes time and experience to build stability into an interpersonal relationship like the family. In short, it often happens in a family that someone is giving more than the other. Husbands and wives and children have to recognize and accept this fact with generosity.

When I hear one partner in a marriage severely criticizing the other my reaction always is: The end of the story hasn't been written. You may give more now, but your spouse may have given more in the past and may give more in the future. True, it may never balance out. But that is the meaning of love, and the person who measures love and attempts to balance it is putting a suffocating precondition on his or her love.

This movement or dialectic in family relationships may cover wide ranges of feeling. Its terms can encompass love and hate, respect and revulsion, overwhelming possession and utter rejection. Whatever the *range*, every member of a family can attest to constant changes in his view of the others. His life is a movement toward mature giving and receiving, a movement which integrates the weaknesses and strengths of those he loves into his loving concern for them. In other words, a person is not in a static state of love with anyone, the love is growing or diminishing. It is dynamic.

I linger on this thought because it has deep bearing on our relationships not only in the family, but our relationships with others, including God. In some sense, these latter relationships which are founded in the family are ultimately more important than family relationships. The family we talk of is not tribal, not self-serving but oriented toward that final giving of children to the world, that preparation of children to so handle their insecurities that they will themselves venture the risk of love and giving in society's communities, including their own families.

In those relationships, it will be imperative to recognize the dialectic of love. A person will experience the movement when picking a mate, when making friendships with his peers, when accepting his social responsibilities toward those who do not share his own cultural, financial and educational benefits. He certainly must know and expect that he will be a pilgrim in his relationship with God. He cannot expect or want a static presence in the eyes of God. He is a wayfarer, he is in motion, and while he can hope to be loyal in God's work, he can expect that this relationship will share all the ambiguity of his other interpersonal relationships. Love moves obliquely, enigmatically; its coherence and direction are, at last, a miracle of contrivances and improvisations.

If this ambiguity is not recognized, relationships with "others" might be rejected at an early stage of development. This is death to the human being. Some philosophers describe man appropriately not as a *being* but as a *being-with* to indicate his deepest need is to develop his social nature. In these terms, his *being-with* is most basically or primarily experienced in the family (as a *we*). It is part of our human nature. By the very fact of the birth which gives us life, it is clear that we are *being-with*.

A New Catechism[1] has expressed this reality well:

If I am asked who I am, I give my surname as well as my Christian name. I am identified by my family. Even something so much our own as our name includes those who are nearest to us. It shows how little we can really be separated from our family. The color of our hair, the traits of our character and the very fact of our existence are derived from others. To be human is to be born of other men, to be woven with fibers from other lives. There was a man and a woman, and a family behind each of them. Two currents of humanity came together in my parents' marriage, and at a given moment, there was I.

But we must rapidly move from the emphasis of this text to make sure that we do not become strangled by a tribal view of the family. While the family is the most fundamental *being-with*, it is not the exclusive form. It is a call; it is itself in a social context. And as we hinted above, it finds part of its rôle in alienating its members from itself as a source of life and security.

Alienation seems at first too strong a word to use to describe the relationship which must emerge between child and parent. However, the biblical image in Genesis when describing marriage ("forsake father and mother") and even Christ's call for his followers ("to leave father and mother") are equally strong. The mature Christian life involves—as does any life—a movement toward the voluntary embrace of insecurity. It is, as we shall see in subsequent discussions in this book, a *human* task. Appropriate to this point is Freud's summary of the task of parent and child in their developing relationship. The child's great task is that of "freeing himself from the parents, for only after this detachment is accomplished can he cease to be a child and so become a member of the social community. . . . These tasks are laid down for every man but it is noteworthy how seldom they are carried through ideally, that is, how seldom they are solved in a manner psychologically as well as socially satisfactory." He goes on to make a relevant point for the Church as well as parents: "In neurotics, however, this detachment from the parents is not accomplished at all."[2]

An attempt for tribal self-sufficiency in the family invites serious neuroses. That drive in an individual inevitably leads to spurning the "other" as a challenge to live and care, and to following Sartre into the solitary life where "hell is other people."

In this framework, the main point becomes clear: The family must know that it finds its strength and its growth as a vital cell by opening to the world—to all that God has created.

A family is open-ended. It cannot hide from the larger society. It feeds the larger society and is fed by it. The family builds society; it is through the family that society grows, receives its new ideas and values.

In our day, society holds out tremendous possibilities for the family's enrichment: With our society's wealth have come many forms of communication, many educational and cultural opportunities, which open new vistas to the human spirit and offer rich sources for the family's development.

At the same time, the family must be protective of itself —it must foster an exchange of values within the "we" that will be strong enough to discriminate between the genuine and the distorted in society.

The family's solidarity with all of society is becoming clearer in modern society because increasing socialization dramatizes men's dependence on one another. Our massive institutions—of business, education, government, food production and packaging, health care and so forth —show the benefits of social cooperation. We have discovered this on the local, state and national levels. We are now beginning to grasp the meaning of human solidarity on the international level: Television has brought into our living rooms the horrors of war and poverty that our brothers of the human family endure in other parts of the world.

The family, then, has a responsibility outside itself. But to put it solely in terms of duty is to impoverish the reality. The family will be enriched by this human interaction —by accepting *being-with* in a larger frame of reference, by accepting the human solidarity that it possesses with all of mankind.

Concretely, an open-ended family is sensitive to all that is good in society: It participates in all that our society can offer. This includes not only educational, recreational and cultural events, but the persons who inhabit the family's environment. The Christian family knows that to the extent that it goes out from itself in concern for other humans and their needs, it will be an open-ended family.

Its home will become a crossroads for people, for new ideas, for new values. From this interchange of ideas and values, the family will leave its mark on the society which nourishes it.

A closed family maintains goals only for itself. It looks to itself as the source of its life, leaving its own province grudgingly to find sustenance for physical needs. It is selfish, overly protective and self-defeating. It is neurotic. If the mark of a family is a true community of love, of sharing, the closed family is deprived of this. Community can come only from a common giving for the sake of goals outside itself.

This need for goals outside the group in order to form community has something to do with the lethargic state of today's parish life. A parish of Christian believers exists to live and worship together with the love of God. But the members of a parish live as Christians only to the extent that they share the mission of serving their fellow human beings in that community. A parish that comes together only for the "liturgy" will be a hollow shell, and "Christian community" will be lacking. Community will come forth as a reality only when these Christians come to be refreshed with the body and blood of Christ for their common work of serving human needs. In a sense, then, a parish is a coordinating center for making known the community's needs, to motivate those who call themselves Christians to give to the broader community by service.

If a parish exists only to maintain its own institutions,

taking the money of members to serve its institutional needs, or if the vision of the parish focuses only on the needs of its members, then it is failing in its primary mission, whatever else it may do. When the Christians look outward, then the parish will be alive, then its liturgy will be credible.

In this framework, it must be said that the Christian family in our society will have to spend a good deal of time working within parish structures to give them a healthy orientation.

This is their mandate from the Second Vatican Council, as expressed in the *Decree on the Apostolate of the Laity*. It is the parish's function to send Christians in service to all men, wherever need exists; Christian families must call upon those who are pastorally responsible to help make the parish outward-looking, must remind them that the parish does not exist for its own sake, must show them that it will be a Christian community only when it serves.

Sociologists have done us a great service in proving that the home is society's primary institution for forming values in children; the family communicates its values to its children. This is sobering to parents and adds a spur to the family's need to form a value system open to the world. For one thing, many parents are inadequate in comprehension of values. We need to refine and reshape our conception of priorities by remaining open to the influence of new information and events.

A child's attitudes on race relations, for example, are

formed primarily in his home: If his parents look on Catholic schools as an escape from the problems of an integrated education, the child will adopt the same values and attitudes. But parents do not communicate values to their child by talking to him in the living room—they do it most effectively by their actions. Values that are talked about but not lived are lifeless principles or ideas; they are not the stuff of life. They are not vital. They can be lies.

We can illustrate the communication of values to a child and simultaneously define a family's role in society. Let's look at a few examples.

If parents are moved to political action because they don't want their children bussed to bring about racial balance in the schools, their child will see very clearly that some of the parents' values count enough to make them willing to give their time to change the environment. In this case, parents will write letters to the editor of the newspaper, they will discuss the issues with friends in an urgent manner, they will get out and get the vote.

Another example: If a businessman is requesting a license to build a liquor store in the neighborhood, and parents get excited enough over the issue, they will sign and circulate petitions and take other steps to block his plans. There are many other examples of how parents—by showing what they consider important enough to move them to action—communicate their sense of values to their children.

In these two examples, the parents are concerned about matters that, in their view, threaten vital interests of the family. I am making no judgment on either case, although I think that opposition to bussing should be handled delicately so the children separate opposition to this possible solution (bussing) from the issue (justice for the minority in educational opportunities). The important point is that by their actions parents communicate and reinforce values in their children.

Values can be communicated in a negative way, too. If parents ignore the needs of the poor—the persons who are straitjacketed by society—if they ignore appeals of lonely or sick neighbors, if they are concerned only for the material goods they can acquire, if their interests are locked into the house, if the extent of their activity is watching TV or being cynical about politics, these same negative attitudes and values will be reflected in their children.

In fact, it is through watching and participating in our actions that children learn most of their real values. If the values concretized in our actions are less than honorable, then even if our family "prays together," it may "stay together"—but stay together with poor values.

If a family in the contemporary world refuses to see its responsibilities for Christian action in the larger society, it may—in spite of its prayer life—be marginally Christian if at all.

What I am saying here is that the communication of values to children, the parents' living of the Christian life, and the person's need for interaction with his environment intimately coincide. They are all one activity. Formal religious education without this foundation of family participation in reshaping the environment, without real concern for brotherhood in the concrete, has little, if any, hope for real influence.

For many reasons, some of which we have touched on here, the Christian family has developed a schizophrenia about religious responsibility. Religion has been divorced from life. As a result, the Christian family is bewildered today when the public acts of priests and religious make specific demands on its conscience. The Christian family is unprepared for this type of wedding of religious values with action.

What are some specific activities and attitudes that a Christian family should generate today? The question is not as difficult as it would first appear *if* we apply here the same approach we outlined in the first chapter: that virtue or Christian response is an attempt to meet the challenges of our day by living the *forms* of Christ's life.

What, in short, are the problems, the challenges facing the man of religious concern today, as an individual and as a member of society?

Parents must develop a mature sense of freedom in today's youth, for mobility has wiped away the cultural structures that supported activity.

Citizens must develop a sensitivity to the challenges

now facing government, particularly municipal government. Cities are the primary *national* problem.

Families must respond to the demands of social justice in our cities with a generous involvement in efforts for better job opportunities, for more human housing, for the availability of educational facilities.

Families must concern themselves with the broader problems of society, of loneliness, of obscenity, of pollution, of hunger, of peace and war. The family must not pass up any chance to inform itself more deeply of the human condition in all parts of the world.

The Christian family today must articulate its understanding of the theology of marriage and the family, so that the Church will never again find itself so lacking in insight in these areas.

The Christian family must courageously reexamine the Church's institutional commitments, particularly to education, and communicate their needs and insights to those who are responsible.

Christian families today must also develop creative, modern forms of prayer in their homes. Too long have we relied on forms which do not capture our feelings in any meaningful way. At home, where the intimacy of the family precludes self-consciousness and formal approaches, experimentation in spontaneous prayer is a real possibility.

These are but a few of the concerns of the modern

Christian family. All of them are the concerns of any family, but the Christian family brings to them a moral seriousness and a hope founded in Christ.

Until quite recently, the standard writers on Christian family life emphasized developing the child's personal morality. This spirituality concentrated on the person's development as a chosen child of God who must cultivate virtue in himself.

In its worst forms, this was a one-dimensional approach to Christian living, which in time became unreal for most people. The demands of this type of spirituality are too introspective, too selfish, and they lead to a compartmentalized approach to religion.

Man is a social animal, and the spirituality that misses that point misses the reality. Man lives in society: His real concerns are all involved in society. That is where the challenges lie, where his creative contribution is needed.

And the other side of this truth is that society is the source from which he will *receive.* His life is bound up with the "other." Through the "other" he comes to the "Other." *A New Catechism* states this well: ". . . it is in the family that the way to the Other begins, who comes to us in all others." And again: "All human life is giving and taking, serving and being served, giving and accepting love, giving and accepting inspiration. Without it, we are dead; with it, we move among new life, new forms, new thought. All that is human, from lonely work to companionable talk or saving someone's life, is in one way or another giving and receiving and hence life-giving and fruitful."[3]

It is in our power to form families in this life of generous openness. An awful power in every sense.

Notes

1. *A New Catechism: Catholic Faith for Adults* (New York: Herder and Herder, 1967), p. 381.

2. Sigmund Freud as quoted in *Great Books*, Vol. 2 (Chicago: Encyclopedia Britannica, 1952), p. 494.

3. *A New Catechism*, p. 383.

6

THE PEACEMAKER

In a time of war peace is a dangerous subject for any-one—politician, social scientist, neighborhood philoso-pher—but especially for the person who wants to relate peace to the Christian message. There is no problem so long as the discussion remains vague; but when it zeros in on the concrete where talk counts, when it is on the level of your responsibility and mine as American citizens, then reason and religion are usually left safely and sadly up in the air, above the war of words.

Let's take the risk. We know we have to. Although we share a feeling of impotence to know how to establish peace in our world, we do know that "peacemaking" is the highest and most essential of the creative responses de-manded of us today as Christians.

One element that will become clear in talking about peace is the necessity for changing *our* attitudes on some basic, even visceral issues. Before we proceed to these attitudes and the actions that the virtue of peacemaking will require of us, the air must be cleared by facing two basic facts that usually cloud discussions of peace.

The first *fact* is that peace—like civil rights—is genuinely related to a very deep need in the heart of all of us: the need to feel secure. We go to war because our "security" or that of our allies is threatened. We establish peace when that security is assured. The problem is that the threats to security can be imagined rather than real. The members of society can be manipulated by fears for the sake of allowing the country's rulers to attain political goals by violence. When this happens, when demagogues shout for blood, the dissenter who opts for peace is a salesman of insecurity in a hostile society. Therefore, especially in time of war—cold or hot—the peacemaker invites society to a risk that it would feel more comfortable without.

Insecurity is not always, then, a sound motivation for violence because of the possibility that the fears are fed by such manipulated hatred, ignorance or selfishness.

The role of "security" can be clarified by an example. Watching the reactions of whites on the South Side of Milwaukee in 1968 when their neighborhood was invaded daily by Negro marchers, you could see many who had fought valiantly in the war against the Nazis, Japanese, North Koreans and even a few who had distinguished themselves in Vietnam. In these wars they had fought for our country's interest but, even more positively, they thought and believed they were fighting for the freedom of other peoples, for the safeguarding of their rights—their basic human rights—in the face of a totalitarian threat. Seeing them now hurling rocks and cursing at Negroes who were walking down a street demonstrating to protest the unwritten laws that deny them the right to purchase a house in that particular neighborhood, one takes another hard look at the reasons these men fought valiantly for "human rights."

Could it be that security was the issue then as it is now? Could it be that the issue in war is not exclusively one of protecting other people's rights, that *many* values are at stake whenever a country wages war?

One battler for civil rights in South Africa, Alan Paton, has said well what I want to convey. Again, the context is civil rights but it applies as well to man's capacity for self-delusion in time of war:

"I had no conception at that age [in his teens] of the way in which man could create tremendous, noble-sounding slogans and could shout them aloud while doing ignoble actions. . . . I had no conception of the need of so much of mankind, while it was actually employed in self-seeking and self-securing, to cling simultaneously to unself-centered religion and altruistic ethics. Nor did I realize that man could so easily deceive himself that his highest religious and ethical values were identical with his own self-interest."[1]

Mr. Paton knows better today. Hitler taught him much, as have his own people in South Africa. He knows today that the South Africans who scream against communism while solidifying the blasphemy of apartheid, the same men who fought valiantly with Britain against Hitler, now feel their security threatened in a new way—by the thought that the black man in the exercise of his rights will usurp the power—especially economic—of the white minority.

Man is *not* a simple creature whose motivation can be discerned in an either/or fashion. If one thing is true about society, it is that it manifests the same ambiguity of good and evil in motivation and action as does everything human. The best way to verify that basic truth is for each of us to scan our week's thoughts, our inner life of motivation, and look at the loves and hates, the fears and generosities, that coexist in us. That test is one that I do not fear to challenge the reader to apply. Only a coward will not face up to the deep ambiguity in his relationships. This, of course, is common material for the novelist, the playwright and the artist. But for most of us it is not a truth we ponder very often in our *own* regard.

Paul Tillich mentions this ambiguity in his critique of Pope John's famous encyclical, *Pacem in Terris*. Tillich argues with Pope John's appeal to "all men of good will": "I see human nature determined by the conflict between the goodness of man's essential being and the ambiguity of his actual being, his life under the conditions of existence." Whatever the theological expression, Tillich's underlining of the basic ambiguity that exists in every man's heart is the only realistic foundation for efforts at peace. "It makes all his doings and all that is done by him ambiguous, bad as well as good. For his will is ambiguous, bad as well as good."[2]

This unassailable truth has real implications for a discussion of the virtue of peacemaker, for it underlines the ambiguity of that virtue itself and the condition of its exercise in modern society. It also emphasizes the inherent insecurity that is man's lot, which we must bear in peace.

Take any slice of history and you will see this ambiguity at work. Seldom are the issues of righteousness in war as clear, for example, as the Allies sincerely felt they were in the beginnings of World War II. The development of that war clearly had its effect on the Allied cause— humanitarian and just. The saturation bombings, the killing of noncombatants, the A-bombs—all were justified as the lesser evils.

There is little that man, the social animal, does without the ambiguity we are talking about. Some see this tension present in our efforts in Southeast Asia where we profess to fight for the rights of the Vietnamese with horrible weapons that kill increasing numbers of those we fight for. And at home, in our cities, there are people who suffer the same exploitation we profess to be trying to eliminate there.

There are clear implications here for the peacemaker. His role in society will consist partially in opening people to a generosity of risk toward others, toward a willingness to see "security" in a new light. This is a slightly easier task today when awareness is growing that national self-interest is closely tied to the developing of other countries and when nuclear war is a threat to the aggressor as much as to the defender. For the first time in history, national self-interest, by force of political, technological and economic factors, is outgoing, is increasingly concerned with the development and security of others.

Another corollary is the need for the citizen and the nation to apply strict criteria to the use of violence. In the case of Vietnam, for example, we must ask whether we are furthering the human rights of those we defend, whether *our* self-interest is overwhelming those we claim we want to help. Statesmen's words, if taken at face value, put war into the perspective of securing rights for others, rights which cannot be secured by any means other than violence.

Their words honor the traditional ethics and rhetoric of Western civilization in which war is directed to human rights as the last means available to protect the human dignity of a group of men.

It is strange but true that it is chiefly in the definition of war that we see the total picture of the role of the peacemaker. If war is a last-ditch attempt to win security for the exercise of rights for human beings, the peacemaker is the agent for using *all other* means for securing human dignity, for obtaining and preserving freedom for the human being.

The peacemaker, then, might support a war effort, if he can honestly see it in the perspective of a last recourse on behalf of human rights. But he will beware of seeing *his own* security above the rights of the other man, he will be careful to apply criteria to all his country's actions and will not hesitate to voice his reservations about the morality of these actions during war. He will also remind his society of the evil and horror always associated with war, even justified war. He will condemn crime on both sides, especially his own.

There can, therefore, be nothing naive or negative about the peacemaker. His desire for peace is not a passiveness that yearns for peace but ignores the rights of other men. His heart burns for justice. While he witnesses to peace and non-violent action, he must simultaneously bring to bear every *power* possible to resist those who would deny human rights to any individual.

We have too long allowed the virtue of peacemaking to be wrenched from its proper context, the establishment of justice. The man who is against communism in Cuba but refuses to be concerned about the human rights of South Americans is not a peacemaker. He is concerned about his own security as he sees it. A country that fights communism, claiming that it is seeking to enshrine human rights, but at the same time is exploiting people, is not a peace-loving country but is using "security" as an issue to cloud its real purposes.

There is a real continuity, in short, between justice—working to make sure that *all* have the enjoyment of basic human rights—and peacemaking. The criterion of determining the sincerity of the individual or the society that claims to be working for peace is the measure of its intensity in pursuing the rights of *every* individual. This is clear for Christians in the context of Christ's Sermon on the Mount where he blesses the peacemaker. For he had just blessed the clean of heart; and he afterwards blesses those who *suffer* for the sake of justice.

This is a difficult vocation. It demands risky involvement in the ambiguity of human existence. It means a man can't simply proclaim himself for peace and then run from life. He must seek every possibility to inform, to educate, to act, on behalf of others' rights. He must forcefully oppose exploitation whether it be Communist or capitalist.

When we talk about peace and war we inevitably realize that to be an American Christian is to assume a brace of special responsibilities. Christian responses differ for the Latin American and for the North American. If virtue is the creative act in society which bursts through the milieu with fresh, new witness to unthought-of possibilities, then the American Christian today has optimal opportunity for his response and maximum responsibility to use his opportunity.

This fact is not easily recognized—even by theologians. I once participated in a theological conference which presumed to talk about a theology of renewal. After a summer of violence—both in our cities and in Vietnam, not to mention Israel—the small group came together for three days of lectures and discussions with three world-renowned theologians.

In the first two days, as we elucidated our theology of renewal in this hideaway spot and talked about building community, it occurred to some of us that here was a world that was ephemeral and irrelevant, a beautiful, logical construct turned in upon itself. It did not touch ground. Not once was there a reference to American problems or to the needs of Christians and Americans in our land; no mention was made of specific challenges facing citizens in the most powerful country in the world, a country involved in internal bloodshed, a country fighting a bloody, agonizingly ambiguous war in Asia. Instead, it was a theology of the make-believe, a comforting, modern theology of community that ignored the larger society while concentrating on the contemporary theological niceties. For example, although 14 men had tragically been killed while skydiving only a few miles away, prayers at Mass were for reunion with the Patriarch Athenagoras and our Orthodox brethern—a worthy prayer. No prayers for the skydivers.

Our conference had forgotten that Christ's call is a rallying cry to his people, a call of urgency here and now. In our time, it is the call for the peacemaker. Kenneth Boulding expressed the intensity of the urgency when he remarked that the human race—to survive—will have to change its thinking more in the next 25 years than it has in the last 25,000.

The need to change its ways applies to all mankind, the Christian above all. Too long have we distorted Christ's message and forms of life to allow for what was in the Church's temporal interest, for what favored a national group. The tradition of violence in God's name extends not only to the Crusades but to our own day. At the Second Vatican Council, some bishops argued for a position more in line with nationalistic goals than with the message of Christ.

The spur to change is, of course, what Karl Jaspers calls "the Fact"—the danger of nuclear war. But effective peacemakers, as kindred spirits, must link themselves together in groups, since working for the elimination of war, as Dr. Jerome Frank has said, "requires the espousal of group values which contradict many currently dominant ones."[3]

It is fortunate that there are many varied groups in the United States representing these values today. Through their work we are now able to delineate, to some degree, which types of group values dominant in this country must be contradicted, which attitudes and structures must be reshaped and reoriented by Christians and others concerned for mankind's future.

Three attitudes, as we have seen, must be present today as real influences for establishing peace: an understanding of the function of "security" in the question of war and peace, bringing with it a need to develop criteria for testing whether a military action is justified or is being undertaken on behalf of a distorted "security"; a recognition of the ambiguity present in all human action; and an awareness of the real relationship between justice and peacemaking, that the peacemaker is the man who seeks to preserve the human rights of all peoples.

Several American values and attitudes hinder the influence of these ideas. There are in the United States many obstacles to the creation of a climate for genuine peace, and we are unable to discuss them all here. I will mention only four. They clearly indicate that individuals can influence society's attitudes, for these four problem attitudes can be changed by work—in voter groups, in peace groups, in education—wherever we can discuss issues openly and honestly.

Some of the dominant convictions which the peacemaker must seek to change:

The Absolute Sovereignty of the United
States Should Be Preserved at All Costs
so that Our Country Can Pursue Its
Vital Interests.

At stake here is a question of human solidarity, a unity reflected in our technological advances in transportation and communication. An isolationism that would pursue goals without concern for all of the world's peoples is impossible. The principle of solidarity which applies here can be seen more clearly in questions of economic significance. We, the Dives of the Western world, are morally responsible for the development of our less fortunate human brothers.

Intimately related to this point is the need for perfecting the United Nations Organization as a world forum with authority to govern the relationships among states, in the words of Pope Paul, "by reason, by justice, by law, by negotiation; not by force nor by violence nor by war, neither by fear nor by fraud." As he said in the same address before the United Nations: "Who does not see the need, thus, to progressively set up a world authority, able to act effectively on the juridical and political plane?" A climate of public opinion must be created in this country which will recognize the equality of nations in the world forum and the need to submit conflict or tension to a representative world court for resolution. The principle of the common good, applied internationally, means precisely that "absolute" sovereignty is incompatible with international justice.

Our Country—Right or Wrong!

This blasphemy of Stephen Decatur must be forever wiped from our lips. The United States itself championed the principle of individual conscience—at least for other nations—at the Nuremburg trials after the Second World War. For others—since it did not conduct such trials for its own atrocities.

Each individual citizen has the duty both as a citizen and as a Christian to form his conscience on the issues involved in government policy and to voice his concerns. This involves the obligation to keep closely and constantly informed about the policy of our State Department, to keep abreast of the types of weapons being employed by the military and to learn, as far as possible, the types of weaponry research we are funding. Special attention must be given to dialogue with scientists, since after their work has produced the monsters of nuclear and germ warfare, it is too late. Witness Edward Teller, the father of the A-bomb, condemning its use. More attention should be given to communication of humane values in every science.

The impersonality of modern weaponry—the rockets and missiles—can lead us to think our responsibility is remote and diluted. Thomas Merton addressed himself to this point in a poem: *Chant To Be Used in Processions around a Site with Furnaces.* The poem is the monologue of a commander of a Nazi camp who was hanged for genocide:

You smile at my career but you would do as I did if you knew yourself and dared.

In my day we worked hard we saw what we did our self-sacrifice was conscientious and complete our work was faultless and detailed.

Do not think yourselves better because you burn up friends

and enemies with long-range missiles without ever seeing what you have done.[4]

Merton is telling us something about our indifference as a nation to the total saturation bombing of Dresden or the atomic bombing of Nagasaki and Hiroshima. As Dr. Frank says:"If there is any such thing as immorality, it is certainly immoral to plan to kill millions of people immediately, to condemn millions of others to a lingering, horrible death infinitely worse than death in a gas chamber, and to blight future generations for centuries to come."[5]

No—even the most *laissez-faire* interpretation of Christian life demands that the citizens of the most powerful and potentially most destructive country on earth face humane men's challenges of the morality of policies and weaponry and research. We must be ever vigilant that our pride does not blind us to our equality before God and our accountability. Even a just battle for the rights of others —as occurred in the Second World War—does not free us from moral responsibility to avoid the use of unjust means and to respect the due rights of all—enemies, noncombatants, even allies.

The Pacifist Is a Shirker or Coward.

A deeply rooted suspicion that the pacifist is motivated by personal cowardice pervades most of our reaction to his witness. In fact, so keen is American suspicion on this point that it is reflected both in the texts of our half-hearted laws about conscientious objection and in their implementation. Documented case histories demonstrate that every effort is made to discourage the conscientious objector. Even though the Selective Service organization is supposed to be locally administered, our local boards usually refuse to take action in recognizing the CO status, referring it to the state boards. Why?

A further problem is the fact that in the United States the *selective* conscientious objector's rights of conscience are not honored. This refusal to recognize the conscience of a person who is convinced that the country is involved in an immoral action, not because he objects to all war in principle, but to a *particular* war (e.g., in Vietnam), is a travesty of America's proclaimed respect for the rights of the individual.*

We desperately need the pacifist and his witness in our world, particularly here in the United States where violent action for solving tension is so deeply rooted that it has now been dubbed "an American syndrome." The pacifist stands as a man offering other alternatives to a world that has frozen its vision on a limited number of options. He *lives* the possibility that peace is such an al-

---

* The right of the "selective" conscientious objector was stoutly (but unsuccessfully) represented to the U. S. Government in May 1967 by the late John Courtney Murray. He made it the burden of the Commencement Address he delivered at Loyola College, Baltimore, Md., June 1967.

ternative. We must recognize the truth in the pacifist's values, even if we disagree with his particular application of them. We must, above all, respect the good faith and vindicate the right of his dissent.

From my discussions with military men I know that the pacifist is looked upon as a threat, a demoralizing factor. Unthinkingly, we classify him as a coward. But from the record of such pacifists as Gandhi and Martin Luther King, we can appreciate that this is a caricature grasped by timid people who want complete conformity in society. Would it not have been applauded in the world if there had been more dissenters and pacifists unwilling to serve under Hitler?

Our Side Is Always Right.

Here is a refusal to recognize even the possibility that the United States may pursue a policy for unjustifiable or unworthy reasons, that a particular involvement can be motivated not by clear, honorable ends but by self-serving political circumstances. It is essential that United States policy be truly political and serve truly political ends. The danger is the common American presumption that *our* policies *necessarily* match moral values—or set them. The other danger is that the personal political objectives of a particular politician can unduly influence the nation's political objectives in foreign policy. In the presidential election oratory of 1964, President Johnson spelled out a policy on Vietnam that never got beyond newsprint, although its pacific tone appealed greatly to the voters, in contrast to Goldwater's "hard" line. That mandate was ignored.

The citizen should be vigilant, and press politicians to enunciate their policies clearly. In elections, it is up to the citizen to demand from each nominee a clear statement of where he stands on the issues of war and peace.

Obviously, there are many more American attitudes which must be changed. We could discuss the need for disarmament, negotiated and agreed to by all the major powers, with provisions for inspection. There is the need to extend the nuclear test ban treaty to all forms of testing and to all of the nuclear powers. But basic to all change of attitudes is the need for a greater tolerance of the risk, the "insecurity," which all change involves.

The virtue of peacemaking is not the same as radical, "absolute" pacifism. The peacemaker, though he dreads war as irrational, accepts the idea that war might be necessary; the pacifist rejects war as an instrument of policy. Both vocations have solid ground in the Christian tradition. More important than the discussion of whether one vocation is better than the other, or more justified today, is the realization that the criteria of authenticity are the same for both.

A pacifism without an integrated vision of the peacemaker as seeker of social justice stands in danger of becoming hollow cant. It is not enough to conscientiously object: That in itself, if it is to have meaning, is only a statement of intent. It is a proclamation that "I am dedicating my life to service." It is an extraordinary call, and to a certain extent it ruptures society. Although society owes it recognition in justice, to be credible it must be lived. At times, proclamation is not enough. What is due in justice may demand a more heroic response on the part of the one assuming this role.

The Christian who makes this declaration in the name of Christ is declaring to society: "Here is a value of Christ's life you have not appreciated. I will live this value as a sign that it is a real choice for you as you formulate policy, as you decide your course of action."

But this makes the same demands on the pacifist as on the peacemaker. Even the context of Christ's call to the peacemaker—the Beatitudes—gives us a clue to this response's place. *There* is the complete picture of the man who creatively makes Christ present in society. Peacemaking is impossible without care for all the rights of the individual—including their defense through power.

Note that I say power, not violence or coercion. Peacemaking will always consist in directing power into structures to insure the dignity of the human being. The pacifist who refuses to recognize the need to channel power into structures that preserve the rights of others is something other than a pacifist: His world has been angelized beyond recognition of what is real. The pacifist vocation is to unleash on a world of violence the power of nonviolence, of love. Any pacifist who sees the pacifist vocation as one of weakness, of passivity, should look to Gandhi for instruction or to the life and death of Martin Luther King.

Each of us is obliged to create hope for peace in any way open to us. First, always, is our duty to work for social justice on the local, national and international levels. This includes lobbying for more foreign aid to the developing countries as well as prodding public opinion toward acceptance of a world legal system and a World Court with authority of enforcement.

We can educate people everywhere to the reality that war in our times is apocalyptic, that our automatic systems of retaliation and the effects of nuclear war are fast making war a disastrous alternative for human policy. Scientists daily sound the gong of the horror of modern warfare, but there is still need to communicate this information to every level of society.

We can spread information about the acute social evils of American society, so that a sober appraisal can be made of our government's use of violence in other parts of the world. If our foreign policy is dominated by anti-Communist slogans, rather than by concern for human rights of people—even people who *want* to be Communist—then the basis of our peacemaking military efforts is a sham.

We can build hope by intensifying cultural and scientific exchanges between East and West. The greater the interchange of personal experience, the greater the sharing in the library, in the laboratory, in the scientific, political and economic forums, the greater the possibility of peace. The peacemaker should encourage such exchange, should take part in it in any way possible, from traveling to inviting an exchange student to live in his home. The effect of these personal encounters, if they are truly human, is love. This is the only lasting basis of peace.

The final area for building hope is in the proliferation of legal contracts among nations and people on various levels, particularly the economic. These bonds solidify human relationships in a realistic manner. Any legal bond made in trust crystalizes respect for another's rights.

Obviously, the greatest hope for peace is related to this point. In the United Nations peoples can speak to one another as equals. If we have to concentrate our energies in an urgent time, here is where we should work. The opportunities for each of us to support the UN are manifold: in conversations, in writing letters to news media, in arranging school trips to the UN, in all sorts of educational programs. We should also be active in support of the UN's non-political programs, e.g., UNICEF and UNESCO.

The UN is *the* forum for peacemaking in our day; it is the most vivid sign that God has not forsaken his people. It is a single ray of hope. The saints of peace in our day—Adlai Stevenson and Dag Hammarskjöld—have laid to rest the myth that God works only through the Church. God works through all human organizations that have a concern for the values necessary in our society. It is blasphemy for the Church to direct its energies only to itself and its own needs.

The peacemaker knows the depth of that type of blasphemy. He will provide the necessary bridge to the world—God's world—and, following the lead of Popes John and Paul, he will try to get Christians to stop looking at themselves and to start, instead, making creative efforts for peace in a broader forum.

Notes

1. Alan Paton, "The Challenge of Fear" in *Saturday Review*, September 9, 1967, pp. 19-20.

2. Paul Tillich, "Address At *Pacem in Terris* Convocation," reprinted in *Peace Is Possible*, p. 184.

3. Jerome D. Frank, "Group Psychology and the Elimination of War" in *Peace Is Possible*, edited by Elizabeth Jay Hollins (New York: Grossman, 1966), p. 98. This essay is extremely valuable for an understanding of the relationship of group psychology to war and peace.

4. Thomas Merton, "Chant to be used in processions around a site with furnace." Originally published in *The Catholic Worker*. Reprinted in *A Thomas Merton Reader*, edited by Thomas P. McDonnell (Harcourt, Brace and World, 1965), p. 404.

5. Jerome D. Frank, *op. cit.*, p. 97.

7

HEROIC OPENNESS TO
THE NON-WHITE

Most Americans have, for some time now, been practicing a new type of idolatry—the worship of white skin, a national obsession as sick as the Aryan blond-hair mania of Hitler's Germany. We can see how far this new idolatry reaches by measuring its impact on all the social institutions that make up our American society: It crisscrosses all structures. And the evidence of it is undeniable, overwhelming—the fact of our idolatry is proved. The most recent documentation on America's racism was provided in the Kerner report which probed the causes of urban rioting during the summer of 1967.

What does this cost white America? For one thing, it certainly kills our credibility in the world's eyes—especially when we claim to intervene in Vietnam to protect the human rights of the Vietnamese people. It warps our understanding of ourselves and saps our integrity and moral strength. But more important by far is what white America's self-idolatry does to nonwhite America, to the

Negro, the Indian, the Oriental. Since the Negro has the clearest and best-documented case against us, let's study the elements basic to civilized life—like job opportunity, income capacity, food, housing, and so forth—to see what we've done to the Negro American through our skin worship.

What does it cost the American Negro to have dark skin?

Research of the National Opinion Research Center shows that the Negro pays an average of $1,000 a year just because his skin isn't as light as that of most Americans. We, the white power structure, levy this "color tax" on everything that we sell or rent to him—his housing, his groceries, his interest rates, the shoddy merchandise we pawn off on him, and on every other service or product where white merchants can take their toll. The *Wall Street Journal* has documented these injustices repeatedly.

The Negro earns, on the average, about half as much as his white brother. A recent study revealed that in Chicago the white high-school dropout was earning 10 percent more than the Negro college graduate.

Our government says that people who spend, on an average, less than 26 cents per person on meals are poor; while those who spend more may not be rich, they are not officially defined as living in poverty. By this standard, 94 percent of all Negro children in families with five or more children are in poverty.

The median family income of Negro families is about $3,800. The same figure for white families is $6,800.

Forty percent of Negroes live in sub-standard housing; only 15 percent of whites do.

A Negro youth classified 1-A is almost twice as likely to be inducted into the military service as a white youth with the same draft status. He's also twice as likely to get killed in action—in the first 11 months of 1966, 22.4 percent of all Army troops killed in action in Vietnam were Negroes, although they make up only 11 percent of all military personnel there.

We could multiply these examples by the hundreds, if not by the thousands. And they would all show what we all already know—that our society relentlessly penalizes dark skin. The irony is that we deny that we're prejudiced. In spite of the alarming picture of how our *democratic* society treats Negro citizens, in spite of the brutal reality that emerges from the statistics above and others that prove the same point, most Americans want more police, more riot-ready soldiers, to solve urban unrest. Most of us refuse to believe that riots are screams for help.

No one who can see needs professional help from sociologists to see the Negro's situation. It takes no particular insight to understand that the person with white skin has at least twice as much opportunity in our society as his brother with dark skin. And to date, few of us have openly embraced the Nazis' overt genocide. But if we simply look at the mortality among Negro children in this country (higher than among South Vietnamese children), we may glimpse some of the possible refinements of genocide.

If we would study how societies exploit minorities, then, let us not look toward South Africa or Nazi Germany or anywhere else; let us look at white America, at ourselves, at how we treat our black brothers.

We can't make Christ's message of brotherhood the heart of our treatment of this problem—on that level there is simply no basis for exploitation of the Negro. American Christians *believe* the right things. They will staunchly defend Jesus Christ's teaching on human solidarity.

And to make things more complicated, as *Americans* we have another set of beliefs that ought to protect any minority from the sufferings the Negro citizen endures in this, his own country. Ask any American and you'll get unqualified support of "liberty"—it's a concept found at the beginning of the Declaration of Independence. Everybody believes in liberty for all American citizens.

The same is true, today, of the idea of "equality." It took a hundred years for the idea to work its way into the Constitution (at the time that document was adopted, one citizen in five was a slave), but today there's generous, open acceptance of the idea of "equality."

These ideas of "liberty" and "equality" are the bedrock of our democracy; even the most rabid defender of segregation or *apartheid* will use the concepts lovingly and sincerely. But there is a big spread between these *ideas,* the foundation of justice, and the unjust *reality* of American life.

Obviously, we must come to grips with this spread between belief and practice in this discussion of modern Christian responses to our society's urgent problems. We have to find out why a society whose self-consciousness is still formed by Judaeo-Christian values—a society whose democratic foundations support its beliefs—can let this sort of systematic injustice exist. And we may find part of the answer in some of our old, traditional ideas of how Christians best serve Christ.

For a long time, sociologists have suspected that people in society act for many reasons besides their convictions. The rash of racial disturbances in recent years has forced them to carry out some interesting studies—studies that reinforce what we noted earlier about belief and practice. We cite some of these studies here, particularly those mentioned in the excellent book, *The Negro American*,[1] to give our discussion a firm base in fact.

In Panama, there is a street that serves as the border between the Canal Zone and Panamanian territory. The Zone side was strictly racially segregated for many years; the Panamanian side has always been integrated. Yet, customers could do business on both sides of the street without changing their attitudes on race.

In McDowell, West Virginia, Negro and white miners were totally integrated below the ground . . . and almost entirely segregated above it.

A Chinese couple traveling widely throughout the

United States stopped at 250 eating and sleeping places; they were refused service only once. Later, when a questionnaire was sent to these same places, 90 percent of them claimed that they would not serve Chinese.

In the classroom children pledge allegiance to "one nation under God, indivisible, with liberty and justice for all." On some playgrounds they are expected to divide that nation.

Sociological studies have found that Christians who go to church irregularly are more prejudiced than Christians who do not go to church at all and more prejudiced than Jews. Least prejudiced are the non-churchgoers.

We could multiply examples over and over again; but the main point—one we already know, one we shouldn't be surprised at—is that most Americans have a "split personality" on questions of race. As I say, this should not be a surprise because we are all aware of the ambiguity of the human personality, of the way we are able to hold conflicting attitudes without being bothered by the conflict. This is why Gunnar Myrdal called his massive work on race relations in the United States *The American Dilemma.*

But if we study this point a bit we can find a great truth that may help us in our search for solutions to the problem. Why, we must ask, do people act prejudiced even if they don't feel prejudiced—and to put it the other way around, why do people act unprejudiced even if they feel prejudiced? One sociologist, the late Gordon Allport,[2] said that *conformity* is the silent partner of all theories of social causation. In a society, he said, people act the way they are expected to act . . . because most people find it impossible to "go against" the social norms, customs, laws and standard responses that their environment, their society, holds up to them.

Another sociologist, Thomas F. Pettigrew,[3] cites some studies that seem to confirm this point. White steelworkers in a totally desegregated plant near Chicago—a plant where Negroes and whites shared lockers and showers, belonged to the same union, worked under both Negro and white supervisors and elected both white and Negro union officials—were surveyed on their attitudes toward Negroes. Only 12 out of 151 whites (eight percent) indicated low acceptance of Negroes in this work environment. But 86 percent (130) were unwilling to let Negroes live in their neighborhoods. In the work situation the more deeply the whites were involved in the union, the more willing they were to accept Negroes.

What does the sociologist see when he looks at this tangle of conflicting attitudes? Besides the obvious conclusion that open housing is going to be a hard battle, he finds that there is not as much conflict in attitude as it seems: "The steelworker is living by the norms of the groups to which he refers his behavior—his reference groups" (Pettigrew). And the norms these groups impose on him often result in what appears to be inconsistent racial patterns, because they keep him from applying in one situation what he has learned from personal contact in another situation. More simply, no matter how much he comes to realize *at work* that Negroes are just like himself, he can't accept them *in his neighborhood* because the demands there are different.

Gordon Allport pointed out that just as "it is certainly true that prejudiced attitudes do not always lead to prejudiced behavior," it is equally true that a person who is not prejudiced may practice discrimination—"especially if he lives in Mississippi or South Africa." The reason Mr. Allport, writing in 1964, mentioned Mississippi and South Africa is simply that these are particularly clear examples of societies that have turned general racist attitudes into prevailing standards by building them into the social structures.

The fact that people tend to go along with the laws and customs that prevail in society doesn't sound, at first, like any earthshaking discovery. But if we think for a minute about that fact and what it means, we can see that it goes a long way toward telling us how attitudes are changed. For years, the sayings that "laws don't change people's minds or hearts" and "you can't legislate morality" have been repeated and listened to without question—they were considered as obvious and fundamental as the law of gravity. But social research has now shown them to be far from certain.

For as we have seen, citizens will, for the most part, act the way people around them expect them to act. One of the interesting studies Pettigrew cites, done in New York, had to do with attitudes among white department-store employees before and after the state's antidiscrimination law covering employment went into effect. Questions asked of the same white employees before and after the law's passage showed that many whites had changed their racial attitudes after Negroes had been hired to work in the store.

The same was true, Pettigrew says, of the attitudes of white customers: They "were concerned largely with shopping conveniently and efficiently; many hesitated to challenge the firm, accomplished fact established by the law; and for many, the new pattern was consistent with their belief in the American creed of equal opportunity for all." It could also be said that the law reinforced white employees' and customers' religious belief in the brotherhood of man. Behaving differently, as the sociologist points out, is often the first step toward thinking differently.

We usually presume that it's the other way around, that our acts are dictated by our beliefs and attitudes. But when we hold attitudes that conflict with one another, as is generally the case with racial attitudes, we may need the change of action forced by law to help us straighten out the conflict in our attitudes.

It follows, then, that the Christian who is really concerned about his darker brother's needs will be most effective if he devotes his energies to trying to bring about social change. The Church, too, if it is really open to the nonwhite, will encourage its members to get directly involved in work aimed at changing society's laws and customs. Some Bishops are finally backing up episcopal statements with action. In 1968, 24 filed an *amicus curiae* brief in the Supreme Court on a case which could be decisive in open-housing conflicts.

With this type of emphasis, those who call themselves Christians will meet a real and worthy test of their convictions; but if we aim our efforts only at changes of attitude, if the Church is content to seek mere verbal assent in its doctrine on brotherhood instead of demanding that its members live interracial cooperation and interaction—if we fail to move from the word to the act—we will fail to affect society.

The research we have mentioned holds another message about Christian virtue, for it shows that the human moral act is not as simple as we often like to think it is. It is a strong part of our moral teaching that attitudes are as good or as evil as the acts that correspond to them. But now we can see that a Christian whose attitudes are unprejudiced may act in a prejudiced manner because he lives in a prejudiced environment. Now we can see that action is an integral part of moral seriousness, that a Christian must prove his attitudes by action, and our theology will have to take this fact into account even though it may require a great deal of rethinking of past and present moral teaching.

But this is a side issue, of interest chiefly to the Church as an institution; the central fact, important to the Church's members, is that the man of virtue will concentrate his energies on actions which lead to changes in society's unjust laws and structures. We're not talking, here, about a choice between persuasion and compulsion; we're not saying that the virtuous man will try to force his fellow men to act in a certain way regardless of their attitudes, that he will be content to let men remain prejudiced so long as they are blocked from putting their prejudices into action. Rather, we are saying that it is a fact of psychology and sociology that society's laws affect citizens' attitudes. It is also a fact of political life (in the United States, at least) that society's laws and structures can be changed and shaped through the democratic process. Unless the Christian is to dream dreams in a tower, unless he is to concern himself only with himself and his own so-called perfection, it is obvious that he *must* take these facts into account.

Certainly, he will respect the totality of his fellow men, keeping in mind the aim of changing prejudiced attitudes, for the attitudes and dispositions of citizens are the foundation of any lasting change in society. But although the two approaches—changing attitudes and changing structures—aren't contradictory or entirely separate, it is more effective to change laws first so as to change attitudes than to work the other way around, changing attitudes in order to bring about a change in the laws. When a person obeys a new law he becomes, to an extent, psychologically committed to it. Pettigrew notes that "when a person has behaved publicly in a new manner [in racial matters] and has been rewarded for doing so, he is likely to become personally committed to the racial change."

Recent studies at UCLA confirm the deep-seated character of our attitudes on race. Using questions that had no obvious connection with race, sociologists there achieved an "altrusim index" and discovered a correlation between prejudice toward Negroes and selfishness, between concern for the Negro's welfare and selflessness or altruism.

These and other studies show that the job ahead is huge. So far we have only scratched the surface in such vital areas as fair employment, equal educational opportunity and open housing. The future does not look particularly promising. The best projections toward 1984, which Orwell has made a landmark in the future, show little improvement in these areas, unless we project an ever-growing violence in urban centers accompanied by a proportionate breakdown in day-to-day discrimination. Many people doubt that progress can come that way, and it is safe enough to say that no one wants to see it come that way . . . unless that is the only way it *can* come.

That's why we call this virtue a "heroic openness" in the nonwhite—"heroic" because each man of Christian concern will have to pull the load for many people too indifferent to budge from their self-idolatry. Sure, they will give lip service to the idea, but real work to bring it about will be lacking. Eric Hoffer gives an excellent image of this response in the Russian landowner who said: "Finding nothing worthy of my attachment either among women or among men, I have vowed myself to the service of mankind."[4] Those Christians among us who are too busy loving God in the church to be bothered with the Negro in the slums are as ridiculous as the Russian landowner.

Notes

1. I rely in this chapter for sociological interpretation on the excellent studies on "The Negro American" published in *Daedalus*, Proceedings of the American Academy of Arts and Sciences, Vol. 94, No. 4, Fall, 1965. These proceedings were later published in book form, *The Negro American*, ed. by Talcott Parsons and Kenneth B. Clark (Boston: Houghton Mifflin, 1966). The edition I have used is the *Daedalus* publication.

2. Gordon W. Allport, "Prejudice: Is It Societal or Personal?" in *Religious Education*, Vol. 59, No. 1, January-February, 1964, pp. 20-29.

3. Thomas Pettigrew in *Daedalus*, Proceedings of the American Academy of Arts and Sciences, Vol. 94, No. 4, Fall, 1965, pp. 978, 990, 991.

4. Eric Hoffer, *The Ordeal of Change* (New York: Perennial Library, Harper & Row, 1963), p. 74.

8

DIALOGUE—
THE RISK OF CHANGE

Most of us nontechnical readers tend to skip past graphs and charts—sometimes at our own peril. We feel, I suppose, that the real stuff of life doesn't show up in statistical measurements, even when these are reduced to curves and bars and lines on a graph. But, while certain social facts require no demonstration, there are several statistical curves with dramatic implications for us as American citizens.

In the last 20 years, certain curves—those representing radio and TV sets, phone installations, automobiles, air travel (in short, every type of communicator or transporter)—have risen incredibly. Today the United States has the most sophisticated communications network in the world. Combined with this is the information explosion, the geometric growth of our information about every aspect of reality. According to Joseph Wilson, chairman of the board of the Xerox Corporation, "these curves together show that our accumulated experience has changed as much since the 19th century as our Victorian ancestors' experience had changed from that of men on the threshold of historic time."[1]

In spite of this, human solidarity and understanding stumble along on the precipice of nuclear war. American city life is ripped by racial riots. International relationships are sundered by war. There seems to be little meaningful dialogue anywhere to solve the problems.

We don't have statistical tools, other than polls, to show the intensity of dialogue in the United States; but two of our most perceptive observers have recently spoken to this question, and their comments are worth noting here. Walter Lippmann, reviewing the nation's response to the Vietnam war and President Johnson's policies, remarked in *Newsweek* that "it is a bad and dangerous situation when a great power in this anarchic world finds itself without leadership which it fully trusts and in which it has confidence."[2] Another astute observer, Norman Cousins, Editor of the *Saturday Review,* has noted that growing opposition to the Vietnam war among American citizens is largely due to an increasing awareness that there is a huge gap between the announced objectives and the policies that our government is actually following. He says: "The government's own policies, its contradictions, its lack of continuity or consistency, its squandering of the moral resources of the American people, and its disregard bordering on contempt for the instinct of Americans to find their way through to the truth—all this is what is creating division at home."[3]

Examples of the general breakdown of communication, both internally and externally, are manifest. Our government denied that it was planning to bomb depots near Hanoi and Haiphong; a few weeks later it bombed them. Our government denied that it was planning a "fence" between North and South Vietnam; within six months it began building that barrier. We claim we want dialogue with China. Instead, we violate her air space, we limit talks to a trickle in a Warsaw villa, and oppose the admission of China to the UN. We also drop bombs 46 miles from her border. We claim we want to "fight poverty," but our legislators and members of the administration are choking off funds from programs to help our city poor and diverting them for more guns. We call America the land of the free, yet we let structures of discrimination stand legally even though they are immoral and undemocratic. While the chart of our technical ability to communicate with each other shoots upward, a graph showing our actual communication and dialogue—among ourselves and with others—would drop off the page.

Many factors work to break down communication within our society. An obvious cause is faulty politics—our leaders share information with us only when the political time is ripe for doing so. A large part of the present racial crisis is due to historical factors and structures that have effectively kept most Americans from coming into contact with minority groups suffering in the shadow of our affluence. Ever present, also, is the real ambiguity of human relationships—both good and bad inhere in man's will, and express themselves in exchanges and contacts that are less than frank or open: We build our shells, and shut other people and their needs outside.

Since we are talking about dialogue in the midst of a discussion of modern-day virtue, there is a case history that seems especially apt. A certain institution, long seen as a rigid protector of traditional values and a bastion of conservatism, has been thought never to change its mind since it sees itself as being in total unbending possession of the truth. I am, of course, speaking of the Catholic Church, whose efforts for dialogue in our time may offer some valuable insights into the situation of the United States today.

Committed by its nature to serving the world, the Church found itself cut off from any hope of communicating with vast numbers of the world's people because of unhealed wounds of separation and frozen attitudes. Founded by the master of love and openness, it discovered that its laws and customs had become straitjackets rather than invitations to free, loving action. Authoritarianism and paternalism had strangled communication at every level; unhealthy emphases on some aspects of her mandate at the expense of others had thrown sound and good values out of perspective. There is no need to pile example upon example, for we are all familiar with the tremendous need for dialogue that existed in the Catholic Church prior to Pope John's papacy. And if the need was great internally, it was even greater with respect to the Church's communication with the world, whose needs and concerns seemed to have passed by the Vatican unnoticed. The Church had to establish sincere, open contact with other Christians, with Jews, with other non-Christians, with atheists, with all men of good will.

How this openness and exchange of ideas took root and grew in the Church may, if we examine it closely, show us the road to dialogue in America at this critical hour. The beginnings of dialogue in the Church have already shown many results, but we shall concentrate on only two areas.

Perhaps the best example of the need for dialogue is the Church's theology of marriage, particularly the development this theology has undergone in our own time. Up until the last three decades, the Church's main emphasis in married life was on the procreation of children. Largely because of dialogue with persons committed to emphasizing other values, the Church has come now to balance its values in the theology of marriage. There is more emphasis on married love between the spouses, on educating offspring and bettering the present human life, in a framework of more parental freedom in planning children.

Both the *Constitution on the Church in the Modern World* and *Populorum Progressio* enunciate the principle of responsible parenthood, a teaching which clearly reflects a new balance of values in the Church's theology of marriage.

John T. Noonan, author of *Contraception*,[4] describes this change in the Church's attitudes in a historical context:

When Planned Parenthood emerged as a strong international movement in the 1920's it focused primarily on the moral implications for society of population pressures, and on the moral implication for the person of undesired offspring. It encountered the opposition of the Catholic Church, which, with a longer historical experience, set out a rule of action reflecting an older balance and a fuller range of concern. The intensity of the conflict resulted from the strong moral convictions on both sides.[5]

Today we can see how the Church's understanding of marriage has changed and grown by facing and considering the conflicting values of such organizations as Planned Parenthood. That dialogue has not yet come to its conclusion, since the Church has yet to develop an adequate theological answer to the question of contraception. But it is important to note that the Council taught that the individual is ultimately responsible for deciding how many children to have; that parents have a duty to consider social needs in making the decision of parenthood; that existing offspring have a right to be respected from the moment of conception, and that this right includes their right to be fully educated; and that marital intercourse has no meaning without marital love.

We have been emphasizing here the values that the Church received from its confrontation with Planned Parenthood. Actually, ideas about the social values involved and their priority have passed both ways, although to date the Church has been less cogent in communicating values to Planned Parenthood than vice versa. The Church's emphasis on life, personal dignity and love needs constant reiteration in all forums of Planned Parenthood.

We could document many other areas in which the Church has profited by dialogue, including the admirable blend of values relating to the rights of conscience that can be found in the *Decree on Religious Freedom* published during the Council. That decree enshrines the individual's freedom of conscience to worship God as he sees fit—a value brought, through people like the late Father John Courtney Murray, from the vital reality of such freedom in the American Constitution. No one can deny that, throughout the Church's long history, it often lost sight of this value.

The future will see the same dignity given to the Christian's conscience in its relation to authority in the Church. Most likely, this development will be along the lines of our American safeguards of due process and the right to a hearing before one's peers—badly needed within the Church as many cases amply demonstrate.

Even more significant for Americans than the Church's dialogue with those who have insights to offer on the topic of marriage and the family are its attempts to open meaningful discussion with the Communists, hitherto the Church's arch foe in this century. Christianity suffered deep wounds at the hands of the revolutionaries, and it is no wonder that some of the scars still show. From the early part of this century to the end of Pope Pius XII's reign, the Red menace dominated the defensive and condemnatory social documents that emanated from the Vatican—and the denunciations produced in that era are profusely quoted by entrenched and bitter anti-Communists within the Church to this day.

Pope John began the thaw by recognizing and acknowledging that changes in sociological and historical realities bring corresponding changes in ideology. By nature a gentle man of dialogue, he concentrated on communism's progressive aspects, its humane elements, and sought to build dialogue on that basis.

Part of his motivation, no doubt, was his consciousness of the horror of nuclear war. Norman Cousins insists that Pope John was not a naive man: "Far from being remote or detached from the hard realities of the present world struggle, the pope knew where those realities point. Men must distinguish between old realities that lead to a dead end and new realities that can lead to a creative and safe existence for the human community."[6]

It is safe to assume that Pope John's approach to Communists was motivated by the same humble spirit of repentance that marked his approach to the Jews and separated Christians. Endowed with a marvelous sense of history, he had the humility and honesty to recall the Church's sins against the Jews, against Orthodox Christians and against the Protestants who left the Church in the 16th century. He recognized that the Church entered dialogue with these various groups stained with blood and blasphemy; he knew that atheism is often simply a rejection of false concepts of God; he knew that there are values in communism that can be integrated into the Christian life.

But the most significant side of Pope John's dialogue with the Communists was his insistence on speaking on a human level about human concerns. Here we find dialogue aimed at the human concerns of our world, at the concerns shared by men of good will everywhere, be they Communist or capitalist. The encyclicals of John, and Paul's *Populorum Progressio,* stripped the discussion of its nationalistic rhetoric, laid bare the human problems of contemporary man for all to see, with the clarity of a humanism that transcends any political dogma. That is why the Peace on Earth Convocations in New York and Geneva were able to achieve even their minimal success. Pope John was not bargaining for any political end. His concern was man's material and spiritual needs. That is the only true focus for dialogue. That is the only level on which it has any chance to thrive.

Pope John entered that dialogue fully aware that the Church had legitimate grievances against the Communists; but he set these to one side, knowing that his intramural concerns would be satisfied if his first responsibility succeeded, and that satisfied or not, they must not hinder the Church's fresh interest in the world, including the vast Communist world. The Church's privileges are not significant in the course of history.

There is solid evidence that Pope Paul is continuing this dialogue with the Marxists, and his marvelous *Populorum Progressio* shatters capitalist nations' stereotypes about economic development and extends their responsibility into areas far beyond their present moral vision. His attempts at dialogue with all the world, of all ideologies, have taken him before the General Assembly of the United Nations in an appearance that will rank as one of the Church's moments of true grandeur in its dialogue with history.

This openness to the Marxists is essential for many reasons, and thawing out frozen Western attitudes is by no means the least of these. Harvey Cox has noted that the rhetoric that bills the Cold War as a "duel to the death between God and atheism" has done more to turn the global confrontation between East and West into a bitter grudge match than anything else. "Nothing so adds danger to the Vietnam war," he points out, "as the twisted misconception of it into an Armageddon between the knights of Christian civilization and the dragons of godlessness. Propagandists of the Church and of the various Communist Parties have stoked the fires of frenzy without ceasing. One reason why Americans find it so difficult to think rationally about world revolution is that they have been fed so long on the strident anticommunism of the American Churches."[7]

Two obvious benefits the Church has received from its dialogue with Marxists are enrichment of its social teaching and improved status for religious freedom in Communist countries. Of special interest is the influence on social teaching, bringing the Church face to face with the revolutionary and radical roots of its social message. It has focused our eyes on the realities of human yearnings right now, a healthy focus for a Church which has long been a spectator in the struggle for human rights.

American Christians can find several approaches to our nation's needs in this study of the Church's belated discovery of dialogue, not merely teaching the world but learning from it.

First, we must enter dialogue with an openness that recognizes that our own values are not necessarily properly balanced or complete. For example, in an earlier chapter we documented the fact that the right to private property—a value Americans hold sacred—is not an absolute right, that it is modified by the prior, and at times preemptive, claims of the human family's common good. Also, Americans feel strongly about the theoretical dictum that "every man should work to take advantage of opportunities within American democratic society"; but this principle can be only half true, if that, so long as society maintains structures which bar a man's development.

Secondly, the attempt at dialogue presupposes a willingness to forego short-term goals, or self-interested desires, for the sake of the real concerns at stake. In other words, dialogue must center on the real human problems and concerns, not on our national goals. For example, the only sound basis for discussing an end to the war in Vietnam is not saving the face of U.S. policy, but insuring the welfare of the Vietnamese people—both North and South.

Thirdly, we should enter dialogue with enthusiasm and confidence and trust. No one person or government possesses all of the truth in any given situation.

Fourthly, we must enter into dialogue ready to modify our position, for no one enters a dialogue sincerely and comes out unchanged. Again, we see the call to "insecurity" which enters into all virtues of the modern man. Few things hit closer to a person's security than the call to shift his values, to open up and look at reality through another's eyes, to revise and update his convictions.

Although Pope John and, to a degree, Pope Paul have offered Christians leadership in these areas, it is interesting that these ideas have not come to the United States through American church leaders but rather through such men as Adlai Stevenson, Robert Hutchins, Norman Cousins and men of similar stature in our society. Americans were directly called to this virtue of dialogue by a U.S.

Senator in one of the most relevant speeches delivered in our Senate in modern times.

On a day when that forum was almost empty, Senator J. William Fulbright gave an historic speech, later published under the title *Old Myths and New Realities*,[8] in which he pinpointed some American tendencies that endanger dialogue. All of us should consider the points he raises:

We tend to look at the world and ourselves in moralistic terms, rather than empirical terms. "We are predisposed to regard any conflict as a clash between good and evil rather than as simply a clash between conflicting interests." Naturally, we see our own interest as the forces of "good." We are also inclined to identify freedom and democracy with the way in which we practice them in America—with capitalism, federalism and the two-party system, "which are not moral principles but simply the preferred and accepted practices of the American people." We tend to consider many other notions—some of them quite mistaken—as self-evident truths: not only about "life, liberty and the pursuit of happiness" but about many other personal and public issues. "Just as the President resides in Washington and the Pope in Rome, the Devil resides in Moscow." (Some would change that today to Peking or Hanoi.) We freeze these various "self-evident truths" into unquestionable articles of faith which become slogans, nostrums and rallying cries in American politics. In spite of all our new instruments for measuring social and ideological change, we rely on outdated tools, thereby letting objective reality pass us by. And when a complex and fluid world meets us face to face, we are reluctant to adapt ourselves to it. In short, we don't want to take the risk of examining our own values in the light of what other people say and think and feel. We like the security of our values as they are, and we think that they're best for us and for everyone.

Senator Fulbright calls us to "think the unthinkable," to clear our minds of old prejudices and do some fresh thinking and reevaluating of long-standing ideas and commitments in the light of new and changing realities. "We must dare to think about 'unthinkable things,' because when things become 'unthinkable,' thinking stops and action becomes mindless. If we are to disabuse ourselves of old myths, and to act wisely and creatively upon the new realities of our time, we must think and talk about our problems with perfect freedom, remembering, as Woodrow Wilson said, that 'The greatest freedom of speech is the greatest safety because, if a man is a fool, the best thing to do is encourage him to advertise that fact by speaking.'"

We have made some progress—in the treaty banning nuclear tests, in reducing tension between the USSR and the USA, in creating new trade agreements with the countries of Eastern Europe and in renewing cultural exchanges with the Communist bloc. Yet our current situation on both the domestic and the foreign fronts will show us that the task that remains is tremendous.

It can hardly be necessary to underline the individual American citizen's obligation to respond to the call and to encourage dialogue on these issues on every level.

Notes

1. Joseph C. Wilson, "The Knowledge Explosion—What Does It Mean?" in *Ave Maria*, February 11, 1967, p. 6.

2. Walter Lippman, in his column "Tax Revolt" in *Newsweek*, Vol. LXX, No. 17, October 23, 1967, p. 25.

3. Norman Cousins, in *Saturday Review*, September 9, 1967, p. 22.

4. John T. Noonan, *Contraception* (Harvard University Press, 1965).

5. This quote is from an unpublished address delivered before the Planned Parenthood Conference at the Hotel Roosevelt, New York City, October 26, 1966.

6. Norman Cousins, "A Declaration of Independence" in *Present Tense, An American Editor's Odyssey* (McGraw-Hill, 1967), p. 473.

7. Harvey Cox, *On Leaving It to the Snake* (Macmillan, 1967), p. 76.

8. Senator J. William Fulbright, *Old Myths and New Realities* (Randon House, A Vintage Book, 1964), pp. 6, 7, 8, 45.

9

THE RESPONSIBILITY
TO BE ALIVE

Karl Marx was convinced that religion alienated men from
the realities of this world, which it downgraded and dis-
missed, that it drew them instead toward extraterrestrial
bliss, a fulfilled life after death. And Christianity goes a
step further. He cited the Christian claim that suffering
on earth is the key to eternal happiness, and that even on
earth man can, through prayer and meditation, establish
an intimate contact with God. As Marx saw it, this dulled
man's sensitivity to the human problems that desperately
needed to be solved: religion sugared the bitterness of the
exploited and smothered ferment—it cut off life.

History proves Marx right to the extent that he put his
finger on a distortion of Christ's teaching that religion can
and too often does propagate. A quick reading of the history of Christianity shows clearly that the heresy that the
world is evil has persisted throughout the entire life of the
Church. There is a persistent tendency to divorce religion
from life, especially from the harsh responsibility to alleviate social injustice.

We have in our time every reason to expect that this ostrich posture will be abandoned by believers. The conciliar documents as well as most recent papal encyclicals call the Christian to intense involvement with the concerns of this life. And there have been strides in this direction. However, as I mentioned in the introductory chapter, we seem to be entering a twilight zone in our dialogue with reality. By some strange process, Vatican II appears responsible for the latest historical and quite subtle brand of Catholic vanity, preoccupation with its own attire. Given its history of elaborate dress, eventual preoccupation with attire was inevitable, but the Church now faces the very real possibility of becoming an addicted lingerer in this twilight area. This preoccupation is of concern to us, obviously, because a prolonged rushing to and fro in the twilight zone of a non-problem will mean more history passed by and more human beings and their needs passed by.

I mention this problem not only because I think Marx has unfortunately been justified historically and sociologically, but also because Christian insensitivity to human existence *now* could prove the pivotal negative factor in man's future. For millions of men, the problems we have been discussing are not remote abstractions. Unless we are mobilized to a decisive response, tonight will mean hunger and death for millions more. The key to really caring about these problems is forged by our profoundest attitudes toward life. Our religious leaders must use dramatic and extraordinary means today to persuade us to accept the privilege and responsibility of being fully human, fully alive. The urgency of this task offers an insight into what it really means to be a follower of Christ in the 20th century.

How, in fact, did Christ alter human "life"?

The "Christ-event" is a life-giving explosion in the history of mankind. Christ imparted new life, renewed old life, gave us life more abundant than we had ever dreamed of. Life flowed through him to the sick of body, to the sick of soul, even to the dead. With him came a new excitement, a new responsibility for human existence, for his Resurrection—erasing even the finality of death so that man can enjoy life—was the sign of death's defeat.

But we forget Christ's victory over death and celebrate instead his sufferings. Missing the meaning of the resurrected joy, we still see death as a constant presence, a threat to our very existence, a looming, dark factor in all human affairs. Terminating our human life as we know it, death sums us up, cuts us off from reality.

We try to cushion ourselves against facing the brute fact by keeping it at the back of our minds. Ironically, we also try to cushion ourselves against its shock by experiencing degrees of death while we live, by shunning our responsibility to be alive, by saying "no" to life through boredom, dullness and other forms of living intellectual death.

Life is a central theme of Christian theology. Through

Baptism the Christ-follower symbolically dies in the sacramental water, to be reborn in divine life, a life of participation in the vibrant love of the Trinity. This new state is radically different from his former, pre-Baptism condition. He is the "new man," able to complete his being and to reach a more satisfying union with God's life through fully living the Christian mysteries. This theology of life is particularly developed in the Gospel of St. John, and it is there that we can see its meaning for us.

The "life" Christ gives is a liberation from fear of the forces of darkness and death; it unleashes man's being and enables him to take possession of himself as a free man living in time, a man who can live life to its fullest. Christ's call is to "life," not to death; it calls us to celebrate the heights and depths of human existence, the joys as well as the sufferings.

Too often in history, we have emphasized a narrow concept of mortification together with an unhealthy individualism; these have led us to see the Christian life in a distorted way, as a struggle to save one's soul, as an exercise in killing one's self, as the business of storing up "divine life" or "grace" for personal perfection. Unfortunately, this idea of "hoarding" God's life like a precious commodity, given to an individual to keep until the day of the final accounting at death, has been the bedrock of our spirituality for some time. Making this spirituality even more unhealthy were, first, a concept of grace that limited God's action to formal ecclesial rites (Mass and the sacraments) and, second, a mechanistic view of the sacraments developed in a poorly understood speculative theology.

One simply proclaimed his belief and then participated in a sacred rite, and—*ex opere operato, by the very action of participation*—God's life flowed through this exclusive channel into the receiving person. It was then the recipient's duty to protect this life, usually by withdrawing from the world's blandishments. I would not say that this description is a caricature. In fact, I think that it's a rather benign description of the catechesis of our childhood.

The chief problem with this theology of the Christian life is that it is selfish and narrow and fails to see man as the reality he is. Man is social. He cannot be totaled or appraised apart from his relationships. His responsibility in life is not to focus on himself. A spirituality that calls him to seek directly and for its own sake a life with God is one which diverts him from his work, even while it nervously exhorts him to be sure to "sanctify" that work, as though it were unholy. In other words, instead of taking Christ's cue of openness, we have caused his "life," his "grace," his "strength" to travel a one-way, dead-end course. In our hastiness to establish salvation and a participation in God's life, we have seen that life merely as personally enriching, a personal guarantee of our vitality in his sight.

I recently participated in a discussion with a group of Notre Dame students who graphically rejected this kind of spirituality, claiming it to be out of contact, a "construct operation" and therefore unreal. One young man pointed out that this type of spirituality is the reason why the genuine "religious lover of Christ" today observes Christians deficient in the refined social conscience of the secular man, so strikingly attuned to the sufferings and mysteries of human experience. "He now confronts a secular sensitivity and compassion which is not only commensurate with his own but often manifests itself more quickly, more conspicuously and more boldly in its prudent and practical concreteness." Another mentioned, as a vulgar example of the Christian's self-consciousness, the old saying that "if you talk about the good works you are going to do, you might as well forget it because you've lost the merit." This struck the entire group as a summary of a spirituality that is aimed at self-perfection. A Christian should act not so that he will be "perfected" but so that his brother will be comforted. Any merit or perfection that accrues is beside the point. The chief concern of the Christian is to act creatively, to bring man and his world to redemption in Christ.

Another student read a few quotes from a current popular book of spirituality that describes well the common spiritual heritage of most Catholics. A few random quotes will exemplify some of the harmful, wrong-headed emphases of that spirituality:

"As *overwhelming* as a personal relationship with Christ is, we, as human beings, want and need some kind of fellowship with other human beings . . ." (Italics mine).

How does one get to know Christ, to establish a personal relationship with him?

"The answer is faith. We come to know Christ through the theological virtue of faith which first came to us through the sacramental character of baptism, along with hope and charity."

Other passages speak of the glories of sanctifying grace, of intimate saving union with Christ, in a similarly intellectualized manner, always conveying the idea that man has direct, easy access to God and his divine life. The students challenged the reality of this experience. They properly saw this spirituality as another facile attempt to rob Christian life of its ambiguity, to carve clear roads for human life, to comfort man with a palliative and specious security that will not accept the challenge of caring for his brother. As one student said: "I need and now possess a belief that will heighten and accentuate the mysteriousness and ambivalence I face. *I wish to live, not speak, the psalmist's plea:* 'Out of the depths I have cried to thee, O Lord' " (Ps. 130:1).

I am not, here, questioning the technical doctrinal orthodoxy of these texts; rather, I point them out because they illustrate certain characteristics of the disembodied spirituality we've been talking about—to emphasize elements that need to be rethought.

The starting point of this spirituality, its whole foundation, is a view of man as the self to be fulfilled, the *terminus ad quem*, or goal, of our attempts to follow Christ. In this view, man is not an agent who must perform creative Christ-acts for a good outside himself, to fulfill the world of man and things; rather, man is to be pushed through a tunnel, at the end of which he will bump into Christ. Even if we update this figure, to the "new view," it is still at bottom a spirituality that sees Christians as founding and forming the perfectible community around Christ— forming, perhaps, a larger tunnel, but still a tunnel.

Simplistically, this spirituality represents a detour around man's own life experiences, passing by the biological and sociological (not to mention sociopolitical) realities of contemporary man's daily life. It wrenches man from reality as he knows it and his view of himself as open-ended, dynamic, creative, shaping, outer-directed, active.

Related to this, certainly, is the old notion that we can best gauge our spiritual progress by introspection and self-reflection rather than by consistently and objectively reviewing our human relationships.

Again, this spirituality introduces a very subtle note of finality into our Christ-following, attaching appropriate tags to the finished product: "state of grace," "state of union with Christ," "state of being." It emphasizes our entering, through Baptism, an eternal divine life so much that it neglects the mission of imparting life to others.

Doesn't our experience teach us that human life is not

some static "state" but a continuous, evolving *process?* Our relationships with our wives, our children, our friends and relatives—aren't they, in fact, characterized by mutual exchange, by continual and reciprocal growth, by change? Don't we have a growing knowledge of each other, an occasional alienation, a never-ending shifting between love and selfishness?

I, at least, have come to see that the primary characteristic of all my relationships is fluidity—and I think that this is due to the fact that my life, my consciousness, is really alive only to the extent that it changes, to the extent that it expands by making new, honest thrusts into the reality that I experience day by day. If I were now to do otherwise, to turn into myself, to turn from the variable to the static, I should have to count myself among the living dead. Faith itself—my faith, at least—shares this fluidity.

Another defect in the spirituality illustrated by the texts I have quoted is demonstrated by that incredible statement, "as overwhelming as a personal relationship with Christ is, we as human beings want and need some kind of fellowship with other human beings." This implies that we can attain to a vital relationship with Christ apart from our relationships with other human beings, that the latter are a kind of appendage.

Note that my objections to this old spirituality do not cast doubt on Christ's action through the sacraments. Nor do I deny the possibility of our achieving a personal relationship with Christ through prayer. But I *do* say that our aim in following Christ is not primarily and directly to "become holy," to become perfect—rather, our aim is to re-create Christ's redeeming presence in the world by living the forms of Christ's life today, by making his values present today as options for other men. It seems to me that to the extent that we keep score on our own loveliness, to that same extent we miss the point of what it is to be Christian.

What *is* the point of being Christian? We are close to a tentative answer. That answer must look to the historic Jesus, the man who walked the earth and was crucified. What are the possibilities of human existence that he lived? What is the particular form of his life that needs to be re-created in *our* day? This is a difficult question and I can only presume to suggest a few aspects of the answer. Part of the problem is the elusiveness of Jesus through the mists of history. Also, there is the problem of the intensely personal reply that we must all make to the question. But of one thing I am certain: There are possibilities of human existence that have never been lived in their totality before or since Christ. I repeat, in looking to Jesus we must look for forms of life that can be lived today.

Even these forms are dialectical. We can't freeze them and use them as models for *every* day, time and situation. Each age has its own need for different possibilities of human existence. Each of us must carve out, define his area, seek his need to fulfill. This is a complex matter, one which derives from our very deepest understanding of ourselves. That's why Christian witness can seem to be contradictory. This living of possibilities permits one man to re-create Christ by being a conscientious objector, yet allows another to be Christ by fighting in Vietnam.

The point is that we study Christ to grasp the forms of his life. If these forms are to be present today, they must be lived; thought is not enough. Christ was a man of peace; if that Christ-form is to be present to contemporary man, it will only be because it is lived. Such a demand on a human being may be shattering. Here we see the radical character of Christianity. Such a form of life demands strength, vision and motivation that far exceed secular capacity. Some of the dimensions of the demand include the utter gift of love, the acceptance of persecution, loving your enemy, eschewing finality of mission, embracing failure, rejecting the view of life as a problem that can be "solved," knowing that all social welfare is incomplete and inadequate if it fills a stomach and leaves the person untouched. Living the Christian possibility encompasses both one's personal death and the realization that the certainties we affirm by faith are not known by touch. There are no guarantees; there is an inherent risk. Love, failure, sacrifice are inherent in the forms of re-creating Christ. I linger on these points because any distortion of the Christian's posture toward the world can sabotage his essential work of communicating Christ's values to our society. The shock many Christians feel at the very idea of any union between religion and life is shown in the now-common reports of Christians standing up at Mass and telling the priest who dares speak out on race relations or war to keep his ideas to himself and stop using the pulpit to speak on such things.

But we have so far to go, so much to do, that when the alarmists cry that the Church is already being secularized, we cannot reply with assurances that "the worst is over." Rather, we must answer clearly and firmly: "We have yet to even begin to carry out the Christian mission in the world; we have yet to scratch the surface. Only when the Church and its members are looking out to the world, involving themselves in caring for human needs, rather than looking inward at intramural Church concerns, will we be able to say that the work has begun."

Fortunately, this mandate is clear in the documents of the Second Vatican Council, particularly in *The Church in the Modern World* and in the declaration on the lay apostolate. These documents form the basis of our approach to virtue as *modern man's response to challenges in his society, as an outgoing act aimed at dominating the sociological facts of his environment and changing them, for the good of the human being with the love of God.* Whatever life Christ gives his followers must break forth into the veins of society. Whatever life he gives to you and to me is given only for us to give to others. Burying it, bottling it, preserving it, thwarts Christ's gift. We must not allow ourselves to sin against Christ's life and vitality in this way.

This attitude we are describing—being alive—enters into all of contemporary man's virtues, but it is also a virtue itself and its exercise is crucial in our time. Another name for it could be "enthusiasm"—not the Kiwanis-Rotary Club type that sees glad-handing as the key to success in life, but the zest for life that seeks to enjoy life and to make life better for all human beings. It is an enthusiasm that draws on Christ's life to enrich our world, to bring it toward completion. A strain in our theology that we have largely overlooked is particularly relevant to this virtue.

Christ is a promise, not fulfillment. Christ's redeeming action is tentative, incomplete, still in process. We are to heed the groan of creation and carry it forward toward redemption. And redemption will not be complete until the apocalyptic time when Christ comes to restore all of creation—including man in his totality (even the body!) —to a new life. The meaning this holds for the Christian is not at all theoretical—it is a call for a deep, vigorous commitment to the values implicit in our Baptism, to feed the hungry, to care for the sick, to answer the challenges of the Beatitudes.

I use the word "vigor" consciously because it was a favorite word of a great American who lived this virtue in its literal meaning, the late President John F. Kennedy. The intensity of his "life," of his "grace," could be felt even on television. He was a man who saw life for what it is, the quest for opportunities to serve our fellow men, for chances to do creative things for the betterment of society. His forum was different from ours, but his life serves as an excellent example of living, in our time, Christ's zest for life. Without in any way constructing a messianic myth about Kennedy, we can say that he was a model of the meaning of our own "responsibility to be alive."

10

CHRIST
AND THE LIFE OF RISK

The general who pleads for "overkill" missile sites, the extreme anti-Communist who fights against Russo-American cultural and trade agreements, the taxpayer who resists social legislation aimed at fulfilling the needs of a minority group rather than his own interests—all of these people have something in common, something very basic. What they all have in common is a very deep experience: Every one of them was once a baby, fresh from his mother's warm womb, even as you and I once were. Our movement from nine months of warmth and nourishment into the fresh air of independent life was abrupt, and our first reaction was a loud wail of protest and anxiety. That first wail is essential to human life, for it is then that we take the first breath on our own, the first step toward building our own security rather than receiving it from others. The second breath couldn't have been taken if the first anxiety had not been expressed.

From that first breath, life is a search for security, an

attempt to balance our fears of insecurity with honest, legitimate thrusts toward the unknown. Some of us spend our whole lives looking back to the warmth of the womb; but we all look back, to some extent. Father John Johnson clearly describes some examples familiar to us all:

Does a person ever think, when he jumps into a cold shower, when he is squirted with the garden hose, when a practical joker drops an ice cube down his back, that his shout of surprise and anxiety is a reliving of his birth scene? Does a person realize when he is frightened in bed at night that, as he closes his eyes tight, burrows his way into the pillow, and draws his knees toward his chest, he is trying to return to the "security of the womb"? Does a person know when he feels alone, and possibly faint, even in a crowd, that the deep breath which he draws signifies the reassurance which he felt at his first breath outside his mother?[1]

Feelings of insecurity and security, then, are deep in all of us, part of our fiber. We know that insecurity is essential to our lives as humans, even though some of us go as far as we can to cushion ourselves from the reality. But as one philosopher said: "Even if we could be assured that a lobotomy performed upon us would turn us into angelic zombies with an unmatched feeling of total security, who among us would subject himself to the operation?" Although few of us would undergo the operation, there are many among us, such as the people mentioned at the beginning of this chapter, who will do everything possible to construct "their security" regardless of the consequences to the security of other human beings.

It has gradually become clear that "insecurity" is the major category or theme of virtue for the modern man. At the root of each of the problem areas challenging contemporary man is a clear call to some voluntary insecurity, some voluntary opening to the risk of giving.

—If dialogue is to become a reality, men must be willing to *risk* a modification in their basic values.

—If racial understanding is to be achieved, those who are closed to others must take the *risk* of heroic openness.

—If the poor and hungry are to be helped, individuals and countries must *risk* capital and aid in developing countries.

—If the exploited are to be satisfied in justice, peoples must *risk* the insecurity of changing social structures.

The call to insecurity is a constant refrain. In a very real sense, then, we can see that the call to virtue in our day, the call to Christian responses to the world's problems, is by no means a flight from the more rigid spirituality of the past, but rather a call to a fundamental human solidarity which makes tremendous demands on all of us—because it hits at the root of our being.

This is in sharp contrast to the assurances religion gave us in the past—and even in our day—through popular "peace of soul" preaching. Too often has religion's world view rivalled the womb for its comfort. Too often has it emasculated man's freedom, his very being, in exchange for an institutional obedience that left him indifferent to the reality of his world.

One significant contribution in the atheistic philosophy of Jean Paul Sartre is the delineation of the view of God and man that he rejects. Man, for Sartre, is a totally free, fragile being who creates himself by creative choices. His very being is an utter insecurity, a constant becoming, an endless series of free choices which he cannot pass on to anyone else. According to Sartre, God is man's constant temptation. Man is so frail that he is tempted to construct a being outside of himself who will assume the responsibility for his choices. This God is totally secure, and man shares in that security. Fortunately, the God that Sartre rejects is not the God of Christ, it is not the authentic Christian God. Our God does not give us an ironclad sense of security. He calls us, rather, to suffer, to be frustrated, to give endlessly, to embrace a willing insecurity. "Take up your cross and follow me."

We Americans probably pursue security more relentlessly than any other people in the world—not only in such obvious ways as our purchases of life insurance, stocks and bonds, and other tangible guarantees of economic security; not only in such idle and foolish ways as our drive to eliminate natural, human odors and replace them with sweet, artificial scents; but most especially and acutely in race relations and our peace-keeping efforts.

We had a frightening example of our mania for security when Secretary of State Rusk suffered an incredible lapse and described our involvement in Vietnam in terms of security against the threat of the so-called yellow peril. We will frighten China away from future war, he holds, by beating the Communists in North Vietnam. According to the Department of State's Foreign Policy Briefs: "Asked to explain why he thinks our security is at stake in Vietnam, Secretary Rusk cited the threat to the free nations of Asia from a militant, nuclear-armed China. He pointed out that within a decade or two there will be a billion Chinese Communists armed with nuclear weapons, with no certainty about what their attitude will be."[2] His views, unfortunately, are reflected in the public-opinion polls of U.S. citizens. If American public opinion supports this approach to the China problem, a whole series of options can easily be by-passed in our diplomatic efforts. These options require painstaking work but they hold more promise than a militaristic solution.

But even more dangerous and more indicative of America's drive for "security" are its increasing stockpiles of nuclear weapons. The designer of America's defensive and offensive nuclear systems, General Thomas S. Powers, gave his views on American security at a symposium at the University of Nebraska. In this symposium on "security" he summed up his hopes for the future survival of the United States in three phrases: keep America strong, use space for any military purposes it affords, and develop another manned bomber in SAC to replace the B-52. In the same speech he spurned talks of disarmament and attacked those who would dare to protest our present military commitments. Some clue to the extent of national support for these views can be had by a study of the latest defense measures voted by Congress. It is, of course, the famous anti-ballistic missile defense system (ABM), a so-called "thin" defense which will protect American cities against nuclear attack. The best appraisals of it say it is a colossal waste of money, since the limited "thin" system costing five billion dollars would have to be extended to a system which costs one hundred billion dollars before it will satisfy the military. Moreover, several Senators (for example, Fulbright and Church) viewed the decision as a significant failure in American diplomacy. The substance of their warning was that it might be thin in the beginning but would be thick before long.

We cite America's quest for so-called security in nuclear development because it was America that ruptured contemporary society's consciousness and most gravely threatened its security by manufacturing and using atomic weapons during the Second World War. Since that holocaust, which Pope Paul has called "diabolical," the arms race has spiraled. The new defense system will divert more money from human ends and cause a fresh spiral in the world arms race.

It was America that led the growth in scientific knowledge freeing us from the insecurities of the past, the threat of natural catastrophes like floods and storms. But this growth in scientific knowledge has been matched by our ability to expand such human catastrophes as war to the point of global incineration.

According to our leading philosophers, psychologists and sociologists, "war"—nuclear war—has become the major cause of insecurity in our time. As we mentioned previously, Karl Jaspers calls it, THE FACT of our consciousness. Other philosophers agree with Jaspers and explain our deep insecurity by the fact that the modern arsenal of ABC weapons (atomic, bacteriological and chemical) has wiped out any distinction between combatant and noncombatant. Sidney Hook has pointed out that we are all targets of instant death. Fiction or not, we know there is no human assurance that the accident of *Fail-Safe* cannot happen at any moment, possibly right now as you read this.

In view of this "gift" to the consciousness of the world's people, it seems reasonable that American Christians will contribute something much more humane to the problem of world security than the "balance of terror." To do this, Americans will have to react differently to the world situation. We cannot react to world tension as we react to tension in our cities: with more force, more soldiers, more violence. Just as more violence in our cities aggravates the basic causes of discontent, stockpiling nuclear weapons escalates human insecurity to the point where the final risk taken may well be world destruction. Why are we so "insecure" about our human relationships that we find our security in an inhuman course of action?

Part of the answer to this question may be found in Sartre's conviction that man is unsatisfied with his essentially frail nature in the face of a "strong, solid" world. At bottom, we seek to negate the frailty of our existence, to build structures that cushion our sense of dependence and imminent death. The problems our society faces can be solved only by our willing acceptance of a personal insecurity. The ironic element here is that voluntary insecurity will express itself in creative acts that will further the security of all men.

It is essential to understand that Sartre is basically correct in insisting on man's inherent insecurity as man—we can find evidence for this in many sources. For example, in his masterful book, *Man's Search for Meaning: An Introduction to Logotherapy*, Victor Frankl points out: "I consider it a dangerous misconception of mental hygiene to assume that what man needs in the first place is equilibrium or, as it is called in biology, 'homeostasis,' i.e., a tensionless state. What man actually needs is not a tensionless state, but rather the striving and struggling for some goal worthy of him." Doctor Frankl's experience in psychotherapy has meaning for all of us: "If architects want to strengthen a decrepit arch, they increase the load that is laid upon it, for thereby the parts are joined more firmly together. So, if therapists wish to foster their patients' mental health, they should not be afraid to increase that load through a reorientation toward the meaning of one's life."[3]

The point is that if security is an escape from risk, the risk *can* be reduced—but only by reducing the occasions for living. Man is a risk-seeking and risk-enjoying creature whose life becomes flaccid and diminished by a stale avoidance of risk.

Another element to keep in mind is that we experience various kinds of fears in the face of the uncertain, the insecure. There is intelligent fear, to warn of imminent danger, of threats which must be taken into account and provided against by action. The insecurity of our family's future in case of our sudden death is an intelligent fear; life insurance is an intelligence response. But the man who mortgages his present existence and cuts his family off from present enjoyment for the sake of a burdensome, obsessive insurance program is a fool, but worse than acting the fool, he is responding in an inhuman way. The same can be said of the country which hoards food from the starving, spending billions on nuclear weapons systems and space races for a possible future while the human beings who inhabit its *present* are neglected.

Unintelligent fear feeds upon itself in much the sense that Franklin Delano Roosevelt told this nation "all we have to fear is fear itself." The McCarthy era is a recent rerun of the Salem witch-fear phenomenon. Racist politicians like Mrs. Louise Day Hicks of Boston, George Wallace and Lester Maddox are examples of unintelligent fears. Most insidious are the calls for greater military action in the face of political tensions.

Unfortunately, unintelligent fears abound in this country. Their number and depth are revealed and measured by a hundred polls every day and reflected in the average man's response to the major problems of our society. It is especially reflected in the hate of those faces that confront the drive for peace at home in our cities, as well as in Vietnam.

It is utopian and naive to think that men in society will confront this insecurity directly. It is not, however, unreasonable to ask individual Christians to voluntarily accept this role in society. Throughout this book we have emphasized that the Christian follows Christ when he lives forms of Christ's life today, when he concretizes ideals by presenting them to his society in a lived way. Then society—other persons—can look upon what seems to be impossible and see that it can be lived, that it is a real option or possibility for all persons in society.

But as we have shown, it is not enough for us to just live these values—we must live them in such a way that we incorporate them into society's structures. As Christians, we do not follow Christ for our own spiritual welfare, but for the welfare of others. Thus, our action must be societal—it must ultimately change other people's attitudes, at least to the extent that those attitudes bar some human beings from realizing their possibilities.

Pope John emphasized this fact in his famous encyclical

Mater et Magistra, a papal document that raised hackles in some quarters—including those of William Buckley, who arched his eyebrows and said, *"Mater, si; magistra, no."* In this encyclical, Pope John explained the concept of socialization and said that it is a natural tendency, "almost irrepressible . . . the tendency to join together to attain objectives which are beyond the capacity and means at the disposal of single individuals."[4] We are familiar, of course, with the expression of this tendency in public authorities' growing intervention in the most crucial areas of human life, such as medical care, social insurance, education and so forth. It is obvious that, in areas of this sort, socialization is a benefit—and, in fact, a necessity. Here in America we've seen the value of this principle in "Social Security" and, more recently, in "Medicare." These programs, pooling resources to create a common answer to a common problem, dilute any single individual's risk; the same sort of socialization is also expressed in labor unions, where individuals join together to use their combined strength to help achieve common goals. Unfortunately, while this approach is easy for majority groups in our society, all too often minority groups are left on the side-lines—for example, the agricultural worker, who lacks legal protections in his efforts to unionize; or the Negro, who lacks the protection of equal opportunity, open housing, equal education . . . and in some places, even of the right to vote. These areas are still open to further socialization, and those of us who "have it made" must in justice extend ourselves to protect those whose risks have not yet been incorporated into society.

It's strange that we fail to see our responsibilities toward those left untouched by the present socialization of *our* risks. But we resent these people and complain that they should "do for themselves" what others have done for us. We are born into a society that has taken good care of its middle class; our insecurities are largely socialized. It is up to the Christian man of virtue to extend this socialization locally, nationally and internationally; this is what we mean by "socializing the risks." The various groupings of society are to be brought to share the common risks. Sensible as it is, it is still true that bringing others to an awareness of the values of socialization is a long, hard work that requires initiative and dedication; this is the work of the modern Christian.

The problems we have briefly discussed are discouragingly large. Some of them seem hopeless in the demands they make of our generation, and it is legitimate to wonder if they admit of solution. One thing I do know is that each of us can help ease pain and suffering *if we want to*. Another point I hold with assurance is that up to now, Christians have not yet been asked to *do* Christianity—we have been living on words, words and more words. Often the words of our doctrines were not even designed to be experienced or acted upon. Like so many other situations, it's a case of something that's no one's fault and everyone's fault, but we've drifted away from Christ-following as "action for others" and come to rest at Christ-following as "perfection of self." And now we have to get back to where we should be.

For these two orientations are worlds apart, as an examination of them at the parish level shows immediately: If the leaders of the Christian community see Christ-following as being primarily the process of enriching individual Christians, one likely result is what we have on the parish level in this country today—millions of people coming together on Sunday, unaware of the human needs of persons who live within the parish boundaries. Too few see the irony of this kind of pastoral situation, in which we measure the vitality of Christian life by the number of communicants, and no one measures how many people are—or are not—served within that parish. The parish— busy serving its members and "perfecting" them—makes no attempt to feed those who are hungry, to clothe those who are poorly dressed, to find jobs for those who need work, to care for those who are physically or mentally sick. This, we know, is a Christianity that is dead and decaying—for the Church must be as outgoing as Christ. Any Christian community that dares to boast of its relationship with Christ while failing to serve is deluding itself, for if we *do* nothing we do not possess Christ. What we have is a figment of our imagination, a construct that comforts us in our insecurity. That's not Christ.

In this perspective, the virtuous man in our times is a proclaimer of Christian insecurity to the world—even to the comfortable world of Christians.

Notes

1. This material is quoted from an unpublished manuscript by Father John Johnson, "The Phenomenon of Love."

2. *Foreign Policy Briefs*, Department of State, published fortnightly, Vol. xvll, No. 9, October 23, 1967, p. 2.

3. Victor Frankl, *Man's Search for Meaning* (Washington Square Press, 1965), pp. 166-167.

4. *Mater et Magistra* (Chicago: The Discoverers Press, 1962), pp. 25-26. The translation is based on the English text released by the Vatican. The consultant on the text was the Very Rev. Daniel M. Cantwell.